# THE COMPLETE

# **FINANCE**

# **&**

# **INSURANCE**

# REFERENCE

# BOOK

# THE COMPLETE F&I REFERENCE BOOK

*Copyright © 1991 and 2013 by David Stephenson*

*All rights reserved. this book may not be duplicated in any way withiout the expressed written consent of the author, except in the form of brief excerpts or quotations for the purposes of review. The information contained may not be duplicated in other books, databases or any other medium without expressed consent. Making copies of this book, or any portion for any purpose other than your own, is a violation of United states copyright laws.*

*ISBN-13:978-1492838890*

*Cover Design: Nancy Stephenson*

*The Law Printing forms reproduced in this book were obtained from*
*Law Printing Co.Inc.*
*170 South Western Avenue*
*Los Angeles, CA 9004*

**Limits of Liability and Disclaimer of Warranty**

*The author and publisher have used their best efforts in preparing this book. These efforts include the development and testingof the theories and practices to determine their effectiveness. The author makes no warranty of any kind, expressed or implied, with regard to the instructions and suggestions contained in this book. The author and publisher shall not be liable in the event of incidental of consequential damages in connection with, or arising from, the furnishing performance or use of the instructions, and/or claims of productivity gains.*

# Acknowledgments

Thanks to Stacey Sutter.

Thanks also to Pat Alford at Wells Fargo Bank
and Rich Ebers at Mercedes-Benz Credit Corporation.

Dedicated to all the F&I managers, doing what you can, with what you have, where you are.

# Contents

**The Business Manager** .................................................................. 2
    The Sequence ............................................................................. 5
    The Sales Department ................................................................ 6
    The Business Office .................................................................... 8
    The Service Department ........................................................... 10
    The Dealer Principal ................................................................. 12
    Notes on Notes ......................................................................... 13
    The Finance Office ................................................................... 14
    The Deal .................................................................................... 16
    Follow Up .................................................................................. 18
    Telephone Manners .................................................................. 19
    Forecasting ............................................................................... 20
    Setting Goals ............................................................................ 22

**Forms** ............................................................................................... 26
    Power of Attorney .................................................................... 28
    Odometer Statement ............................................................... 28
    Report of Sale .......................................................................... 29
    Agreement to Furnish Insurance ............................................ 31
    Notice to Cosigner ................................................................... 33
    9 pack ....................................................................................... 34
    Payoff Verification ................................................................... 35
    Leased Trade ............................................................................ 36

**The Customer Statement** ............................................................. 40
    Calculating a debt ratio ........................................................... 42
    Income Verification ................................................................. 46

**The Credit Profile** ......................................................................... 48
    The customer interview .......................................................... 50

**Working with Lenders** ................................................................. 56

**The Finance Contract** .................................................................. 62
    Computer skills ........................................................................ 62
    Why finance through the dealer? ........................................... 63
    Converting a credit union loan ............................................... 63
    Converting the cash customer ............................................... 64
    Establishing a credit rating ..................................................... 65
    Cosigners .................................................................................. 65

> One Pay Contracts ................................................................. 66
> Business loans ........................................................................ 67
> Simple Interest ...................................................................... 67
> Rule of 78s ............................................................................. 69
> Assigning the contract .......................................................... 71
> Documentation ...................................................................... 72

**The Lease** ......................................................................................74
> Questions about leasing ....................................................... 75
> Insurance requirements ....................................................... 75
> Residual calculation ............................................................. 77
> Luxury tax ............................................................................. 77
> Gap insurance ....................................................................... 78
> Lease payment calculation .................................................. 78
> Leasing v Financing ............................................................. 79
> Plan A v Plan B .................................................................... 80
> Business lease ....................................................................... 82

**The Cash Deal** ...............................................................................86

**Selling** ..............................................................................................88
> Be an authority ..................................................................... 88
> Be a counselor ...................................................................... 89
> Be a psychologist ................................................................. 89
> Feature appropriate benefits ............................................... 92
> Context makes meaning ...................................................... 92
> Summary ............................................................................... 93
> Neuro-Linguistic Programming ......................................... 94
> Mirroring ............................................................................... 96
> State of mind ........................................................................ 97
> Body language ...................................................................... 98
> Voice ...................................................................................... 98
> The right words .................................................................... 99
> Connecting words ................................................................ 99
> Embedded commands ....................................................... 101
> Use the name ...................................................................... 101
> Reframe an objection ........................................................ 101
> Handling objections .......................................................... 102
> Ask questions ..................................................................... 104

    Ask more questions ............................................................. 105
    Belief .................................................................................... 105
    Models ................................................................................. 106

**Service Contracts** ................................................................ 110
    Presentation ........................................................................ 112
    Objections ........................................................................... 114
    Benefits ................................................................................ 116
    Forms ................................................................................... 117
    Follow-up letter .................................................................... 118

**Credit Insurance** .................................................................. 122
    Presentation ........................................................................ 124
    Objections ........................................................................... 126
    Definitions ........................................................................... 128
    Benefits ................................................................................ 129

**Accessories** ........................................................................... 132
    Display ................................................................................. 134
    Brochure .............................................................................. 135
    Packages ............................................................................. 136
    Products .............................................................................. 137

**Appendix A: DMV Forms** ................................................... 142
    Demonstrators and executive cars ...................................... 142
    Non-resident military ........................................................... 142
    Statement of Facts Environmental Plates ........................... 143
    Plate interchange ................................................................ 143
    Environmental Plates .......................................................... 144
    Statement of Error ............................................................... 145
    Bill of Sale ........................................................................... 145
    Lien Satisfied ....................................................................... 146
    Name statement .................................................................. 146
    Statement of Facts .............................................................. 147
    Duplicate registration .......................................................... 147
    Duplicate title (front) ............................................................ 148
    Duplicate title (back) ........................................................... 148
    Commercial registration ...................................................... 149
    Title only transfer ................................................................ 149

**Appendix B: Laws and Taxes ........................................... 150**
    Sales tax ............................................................... 150
    Luxury tax exemption ........................................... 151
    Out-of-state delivery ............................................. 151
    Resale card ............................................................ 152
    Tax declaration ..................................................... 152
    Sales tax chart ...................................................... 153
    Luxury tax ............................................................ 154
    Regulation Z ......................................................... 155
    Consumer Leasing Act ......................................... 156
    Equal Opportunity Credit Act ............................. 157
    Magnusson-Moss Warranty Act .......................... 158

**Appendix C: APR to ADD-on rates ................................. 159**

**Appendix D: Schedule C .................................................. 160**

**Appendix E: Deal Forms .................................................. 161**
    Rescission agreement ........................................... 161
    Recap sheet ........................................................... 162
    Follow-up .............................................................. 163
    Weekly log ............................................................ 164
    Call log .................................................................. 165
    Monthly Sales log ................................................. 166
    Income verfication ................................................ 167
    Forecasting ............................................................ 168
    Daily Finance log ................................................. 170

**Glossary ............................................................................. 175**

**Index .................................................................................. 182**

# Introduction to the First Edition

I learned the Finance and Insurance position on-the-job. After my first two weeks at Spring Toyota in San Luis Obispo in August, 1979, Law Printing had to make an emergency delivery of forms. Every F&I manager I know learned the same way. This is surely the only way to learn, but there were many times when a reference manual would have come in handy. Even as I was writing this book, after fourteen years in the business, I would occasionally have to call the DMV, the State Board of Equalization or a banker friend and ask,"How is this supposed to be done anyway?"

There is also so the legendary problem of F&I back-up. Every finance manager has gone through the return-from-vacation blues. The why-did-I-ever-go syndrome. You come back and it looks like everyone came to dinner and left all the dishes in the sink. Other managers may know bits and pieces of F&I, but we have to admit that most sales managers just don't want to be responsible for the paperwork. I thought a reference manual might come in handy at times like those ... when some paperwork needs to be completed, or something has to be explained to a customer ... and the regular F&I manager is not yet back from the sanitarium.

The car business is evolving. The days of grinding the customer into mush are giving way to a time when service is a priority. Of course, the customer still needs guidance and counsel, so that he or she may protect themselves and their new car appropriately against the slings and arrows of outrageous fortune. Pure pressure, however, is being transformed into professional service. The scenes are fading in which an insensitive finance manager pulverizes a poor customer, squeezing all the fun of the purchase out of him and leaving him limp and sweating, to be dragged out of the office by the salesperson and propped up behind the wheel of his brand new car.

Service is the name of the game now. To win, you cannot fake it. You need to mean what you say. Customers may know more than they used to about buying cars, but they still don't buy cars very often, and they appreciate professional assistance. Everybody wins with a professional finance department. The dealer sells more cars, makes more money per car and sees more customers return to the store. The customer gets to enjoy what could otherwise be an intimidating and anxious experience ... coming through a major decision process and feeling good about it. The finance manager makes a good living and meets hundreds of interesting people.

Meeting people is what I personally enjoyed the most. Everybody needs a car. It is educational to meet so many people from so many different walks of life and the finance manager is the only person in the dealership who meets everyone and sees their private lives, their problems and their promises.

Seven years of teaching English and Psychology turned out to be a fertile foundation for a sales career. When I moved to the Silicon Valley in 1982, I was hired as part of the management team at Smythe European Mercedes-Benz, with whom I stayed for eight years.

I left the F&I office to start a business with my wife, Nancy, who is a graphic designer, and spend more tme with my sons, Eric and Alex. This book sums up what I know about being an F&I manager. A reference book, with an index, was something I looked for often. I hope you find it useful.

San Jose, 1991

# Introduction to the Second Edition

There can be no doubt that this book is out-of-date. It is decidedly 'old school'. Even though the laws have changed, the taxes have gone up and the technology is improved by several generations, The Complete F&I Reference Book is still the only book of its kind. In the 1990's, it was very popular in F&I offices all over the country and it was used by many Dealer schools, including Northwood University. Most F&I training companies provided the book for trainees.

The first printing was twenty-two years ago. Since then, much of the car business seems to have changed: the Internet, the Recession and new Consumer Protection laws at every turn. Compliance is the order of the day. When I was asked about re-printing this book, I visited a few dealerships. I kept hearing how things had changed ... how 'talent' had left the business and now it was all about 'systems'. I decided to go ahead with a second edition after hearing a similar message from several General Managers: "... a dose of 'old school' would really benefit this new generation of salespeople."

My own story continued to weave around the car business for another fourteen years after the initial publication of this book. For the first couple of years, I travelled around the country doing seminars and consulting based on the book. And then, in 1993, I joined The Automark Group ... a start-up company out of Fairfax, Virginia. Automark provided customized presentations of the features and benefits of F&I products, displayed on the F&I managers' computer screen. And we provided training on how to make those presentations effectively. In 1993, an installation of one system would take all day and involve a large box of floppy disks. I hauled my own presentation equipment (a 386 computer and a monitor) around in two large pizza suitcases. We provided some of the first dealer web sites, working with the largest dealer groups in the country. In 1999, Half-A-Car became aware of lease presentations we had designed for showroom floor monitors and bought Automark. Then Half-A-Car was bought by Reynolds and Reynolds.

In 2001, I went back in the car business to help a friend get his store ready for sale. Jardine Matheson (of Hong Kong) wanted to sell Beverly Hills Mercedes-Benz. I was hired as Director of Marketing. We upgraded the Internet Sales department and the Fleet department, eliminated a marginally-performing Call Center, created a Delivery department (cars were increasingly complicated and deliveries increasingly time-consuming) and created mutually-rewarding vendor relationships around town. In 1993, the store was bought by a dealer group out of Houston.

So 2003 was the end of the car business for me. It was time to follow my heart. Until last year, I worked as a professional sports photographer, covering the Giants, A's, 49ers, Sharks and other pro sports in the Bay area. When I turned 64, I found it was time to retire and reflect on what I have learned. My second book, Rugby Stories ... and other misadventures, was published last month.

Now that I live up here by the Russian River, deep in the redwoods, it all seems to me to have been another life. Still, the path to living successfully doesn't change. Care about other people, do what's right, don't be afraid to turn the world your way and you will get what you deserve.

Rio Nido, 2013

It is impossible for all things to be precisely
set down in writing:
for rules must be universal,
but actions are concerned with particulars.


- Aristotle

# The Business Manager

> The credit belongs to the man [or woman] who is actually in the arena; whose face is marred by dust and sweat and blood; who strives valiantly; who errs and comes up short again and again; who knows the great enthusiasms, the great devotions; and spends hin or her self in a worthy cause; who at the best knows in the end the triumph of high achievement; and at the worst, if he [or she] fails while daring greatly; so that his or her place shall never be with those cold and timid souls who know neither victory nor defeat.
>
> - Theodore Roosevelt

The Sales Business manager is a salesperson, first and foremost. He or she is selling at every turn. The F&I manager must convince the sales department that the first priority of the F&I office is the deal. The office must believe that the F&I manager is not sacrificing thoroughness for quick profit. The service department needs to know that they don't have to spend their time answering the false promises that the F&I department made in order to sell service contracts and accessories. The owner wants to be sure that his or her interests are protected, while at the same time, no money is being left on the table. Every deal needs to be sold to the bank in some way, not just the borderline deals ... there are exceptions to every rule. Finally, the F&I manager will only make money if she or he can sell to the customer.

While she is busy selling throughout the day, the Business Manager must not lose sight of the administrative and legal responsibilities. Truth in Lending laws, the Fair Credit Reporting Act, Regulation Z ... more and more compliance issues as the world grows more complicated. Keeping the cash flow current, making sure a broker has a resale license, verifying a payoff ... all in a day's work.

The F&I position is truly unique. You are not a car salesperson, nor are you a banker, but you are expected to be both. You must close a good percentage of the deals, sometimes for no commission and still you should average $1000 gross profit per car. You must, as a manager, protect your dealer and yet you are expected to deliver every car, as long as the customer is breathing, regardless of economic status. You are offered no trips to the factory, no cruises or even a weekend at the beach. You are there to call the banks first thing in the morning and you are there waiting to see if that last deal will happen at 11 o'clock at night. And only when you screw up, do people pay attention. Yes. A truly unique position.

It is the most demanding job in the dealership. Still ... you are not the salesperson facing the agony of cold calls, suffering the anxiety of waiting for a customer who fails to keep his appointment or enduring the constant grind that is necessary to find the customer who will buy today. You're not the loan officer sitting on the receiving end of a telephone all day, never meeting people face-to-face and getting periodically ground into dust by a finance manager whose life is on the line. Each deal tells its own story, each customer actually brings something new into your life.

> Desire is the key to motivation, but it's the determination and commitment to an unrelenting pursuit of your goal ... a commitment to excellence ... that will enable you to attain the success you seek.
>
> - Mario Andretti

The F&I job is never boring, always character-building and pays well. In fact, everybody (including sales managers) should have to do it at least once. The most successful Genereal Managers and Dealers have real experience of the responsibilities of the F&I office. They either employ a finance manager whom they trust and believe in, or they are continually looking for someone to fulfil what they know the real potential in F&I.

The challenge can only be met by a certain kind of person. A sales personality, and yet careful with details. A strong, but definitely not a silent type. Persistent and yet able to negotiate, with the ability to judge, but not pre-judge, people. The desire to do whatever it takes to get the job done ... with a sense of ethics. Most of all, a successful business manager works hard ... very hard ... and likes it.

This book will suggest that the most substantial profit is to be found in an all-around approach. Support sales, watch cash flow, meet every customer and ask for the sale. A good F&I manager is in business for the long-term, cultivating relationships, establishing credibility and building a record of honest work. Sincerity truly does sell. Sincerity that just purely takes advantage of people does not sell for long. In the car business, where so much negotiation is conducted over the telephone, your word really should be your bond. Your ability to get deals bought at the bank hinges on your credibility.

When you're selling to a customer in your office, you can be a counter-balance to a situation that is an intimidating and anxious experience for most people. Once a customer sees that you know what you're doing, that you are actually helping them and that you believe in the value of what you are offering, he or she will take your advice, more often than not. You must admit to yourself that you are there to sell and you must give it your best at every opportunity. Otherwise you are just wasting your time.

The key to managing the sales business department is communication. Communicate constantly with the sales department, with the business office, with the service department and with the dealer principal. You need continuing communication with lenders and customers. You even need to communicate with yourself ... not as strange a notion as it sounds.

Make notes on everything you do ... on every decision you make. Document when and where deals were submitted, as well as how and when deals are approved. Develop the habit. Write it down.

> When a man (or woman) does not know what harbor she is making for,
> no wind is the right wind.
>
> - Seneca

Within the space of a twenty-minute encounter, the F&I manager is expected to work minor miracles with people he or she has never met before. Fortunately, the professional has the ways and means to be productive. The game is played on your turf and you get to set the expectations. The customer is looking to you for direction.

It is actually true that 'things' in themselves have no meaning. Our nervous system manufactures meaning from the raw material that our sense organs provide. Context, attitude and timing all affect the meaning of experience. In order to be successful as a salesperson, there is nothing that you need to do *to* the customer. The key is within you. It is *your* commitment, *your* expectation, *your* belief that will communicate beyond words.

How do you picture your job? Notice that you **do** picture it. And then you check that picture against what you think is happening to see if things are going ok. In order not to be wasting time at the office, reverse that process. Visualize 'things' the way you want them to be. And then get to work. The great lesson of all the writers quoted in this book is that the meaning of life is not out there somewhere, waiting to be discovered. It is in you, now, waiting to be shared.

While you are at work, that sharing is selling. You want the customer to buy a decent product at a fair price. It is purely self-defeating to be shy about it. The customer expects that, if you think a product or service is so good, you will want to sell it to her. He or she wants a reason to buy. In F&I, that reason is you.

> *Our doubts are traitors and make us lose the good we might oft win by fearing to attempt.*
>
> *- William Shakespeare*

- ❖ Have the deal in the computer and the initial paperwork already typed.

- ❖ Be introduced as "The Business Manager" who will handle all the paperwork and answer any questions that the customer may have.

- ❖ Establish pleasant conversation. Ask about the customer's choice of vehicle. Comment on something you have in common.

- ❖ Complete the initial paperwork during this conversation. Take care to establish your competence and your authority.

- ❖ Discuss methods of payment: always mention financing and leasing.

- ❖ Discuss the extended warranties available.

- ❖ Discuss insurance, if relevant.

- ❖ Discuss accessories. Inform the customer that you are the one to talk with about accessories, since you can include the options in the contract.

- ❖ Establish value before you dicuss price.

- ❖ Put off all the questions about price, cost, etc. until you have finished all the presentations. "I will show you everything before you sign anything. We'll ask the comuter for the figures in just a moment".

- ❖ Start high when you quote price. Quote price in terms of an increase in monthly payment whenever possible. Never lower a price or a payment without a reason.\

- ❖ Always trail-close a change in rate or payment: "If I could do the contract would that work for you?". Or, "If the service contract were only costing you $10 a month, would that be worthwhile?"

- ❖ Close a finance or lease disclosure on the payment date: discuss the convenience of that date to the customer. Offer to change the date to make it more convenient, if possible.

- ❖ End the meeting with the customer in the same way you started, with pleasant conversation about subjects other than the deal. Page the salesperson and return the customer to his or her care. Do not encourage the customer to wander out on to the showroom floor alone.

## The Sales Department

The difference between a good F&I department and a great F&I department is the sales desk. A sales manager who doesn't give away the rate on every deal is a finance manager's best friend. Too often a weak, or short-sighted desk manager will include a service contract to make a deal ... and keep the gross. Or the salesperson will be allowed to 'throw in' those chrome wheels or the appearance protection package. It is essential that the sales manager be compensated for the F&I gross. You should make sure that is the case.

A good sales manager understands that there are times when a buyer is locked in on price, but there are other ways to add to the overall gross. If the customer is negotiating on price only, the sales manager can make money on the rate, or by including a service contract or insurance in the payment. Every good sales manager in the business does this, but only if he or she gets paid for it. When a deal comes from the desk with F&I services included, be sure the customer realizes the value of what he or she is buying. Show the price of the services and the consequent increase in payment. If there are any objections, that is the time to sell. It should be clear that, if the F&I department is responsible for making a profit on financing, leasing, service contracts and accessories, then the F&I manager should be the one to set the retail prices and retain the profit. Clear, close coordination is vital. Each manager must trust the other completely.

Your salespeople must believe that you will do absolutely everything possible to get their deals bought. Your priorities should always be the deal first. F&I profit second. There will be deals that require a delicate touch ... the customer must be 'nursed' through the closing process. And there will be deals where a particularly firm hand is called for. On such deals, sometimes discretion will be the better part of valor. That is, you may sacrifice a persistent sales effort on behalf of your services in order to keep a deal together. *Although you should always ask for the sale.* This will gain the cooperation of the sales department. It will work both ways. Once they trust you, they will help you whenever they can. At the very least, they will stop telling every customer not to worry about financing because they can always go their own bank.

Ideally, you should be able to provide incentives for the salesperson who goes out of his or her way to help you. The sales staff should be concerned with selling the car, first and foremost. So should the F&I manager. No car sale, no F&I. Once the car is sold however, you want everyone to be thinking of ways to help.

---

You can get everything in life you want,
if you help enough other people get what they want.

- Zig Ziglar

> The ability to deal with people is as purchasable a commodity as sugar or coffee and I pay more for that ability than for any other under the sun.
>
> - John D. Rockefeller Jr.

- ❖ Your first responsibility is to deliver the car and protect the gross.

- ❖ Keep a rate book in the sales office for the sales manager. Update as needed. Keep the desk informed as to which banks you prefer for various kinds of financing or leasing.

- ❖ Hold a sales meeting and/or individual meetings to explain the importance of complete credit applications. Demonstrate key points that strengthen a customer profile.

- ❖ Offer incentives for service contract and accessory sales. Ask the sales staff what they would consider an incentive. Run a contest.

- ❖ While an application is pending approval, let each salesperson know that you are monitoring the progress of his or her deal carefully. If they are not available, leave notes for them.

- ❖ Be creative. Treat the salesperson the way you would like the banks to treat you. Find a way the deal can be made. You might be surprised what a good salesperson can accomplish when he or she knows what is needed.

- ❖ Alert the sales desk when you become aware of an opportuntiy for profit ... a special lease promotion, a change in the buy rate or a change in bank policy.

- ❖ Three out of four people who finance through the dealership will return to buy another car. This is a great support for sales.

- ❖ On those deals where you sense a certain amount of instability, encourage the salesperson to assist with gathering income documentation and insurance verification before the car is delivered. A customer who withholds stipulated documentation has the power to unwiind the deal. The salesperson should be aware of this.

- ❖ Whenever possible, work through the sales desk to enlist a salesperson's cooperation. Resist the temptation to unload emotion on a salesperson who exhibits an aversion to paperwork. However, do not assume the extra burden of doing their work for them. Talk to the sales manager.

## The Business Office

Just as your relationship with the sales department may depend on how you get along with people, the office staff will judge you based on how you get along with paper. If, in the heat of wheeling and dealing, you catch yourself thinking that some little task isn't actually that important ... no registration on a trade ... no duplicate request when you didn't have a title, no printed worksheet on a lease deal ... remember, someone will eventually have to fix that. Probably you. And if not you, someone in the office whose opinion of you will decline accordingly. Dealing with paperwork all day can be boring. *Fixing* paperwork all day can be boring and irritating.

Know who is responsible in the office for packaging the deals and sending them to the bank. Be certain that this person understands the requirements of each bank, or arrange to 'final check' each package before it is sent.

Streamline the processing of a deal. How long does it take, after a deal leaves your office, for that deal to reach the funding desk at the bank? What can be done to speed up this process? Are copies of R.O.'s or Due Bills (documenting additional options) being included routinely? Who signs off on the back of the contracts? Is this being done every day? Are packages put in the regular mail or expressed? Communicate your priorities to the office.

Develop a relationship with your office manager. Not only is this probably the person who administrates your pay plan, but the responsibility for tracking reserves and charge-backs also falls on the office manager. How are the reserves actually paid? How are charge-backs handled?

Check with the DMV secretary. Are the license fees and taxes coming through accurately? How are the powers of attorney being handled?

Make sure that the contracts desk is working from the same cost sheets as the sales department and F&I. Ask to made aware of any differences in cost from other departments. Are the changes in the recap process that would help the office?

Be conscious of birthdays and other occasions that are special for office personnel. Show that you appreciate their support.

---

*The deepest principle in human nature is the craving to be appreciated.*

- William James

> You have to learn the rules of the game.
> And then you have to play better than anyone else.
>
> - Albert Einstein

- ❖ Be careful with the paperwork. If you make the paper flow as conveniently as possible for the office staff, they will help you. They might assist when the license fees are incorrect, when a payoff difference needs to be invoiced or when the monthly transmittals need to be typed.

- ❖ Get to know the staff and the office manager. You want the staff to be looking out for your best interest. If they don't know you, how can they care?

- ❖ Leave notes in the deal that explain anything unusual. "Current registration coming tomorrow" … "Hold check until Monday, December 3".

- ❖ Keep the paperwork for each deal in a separate folder or jacket and note on the front whether it is a cash deal, one-pay …etc., which bank it should go to and what other documentation needs to be included … tax return, financial statement, etc.

- ❖ Ask for an Accounts Receivable list every day and work diligently to keep the cash flow as current as possible. Call the one-pay customer and offer assistance , reminding him what you have to offer. Call the bank and confirm they have what they need to fund. Keep notes.

- ❖ Note when deals are funded and check the reserve against your log. Track down the reason for any consistent delays in funding or significant differences in reserve.

- ❖ Document the dealer additions to the vehicle: include an invoice, a due bill or a 'get-ready".

- ❖ Ask the question of everyone in the business office: "Is there anything I can do to make your job easier or more productive?"

- ❖ Establish a routine procedure for handling differences in trade-in payoffs. Call the cusomer yourself if there is money to be collected after you have verified the payoff. And ask the office to mail an invoice.

- ❖ Be certain that the person in the office who is responsible for packaging the deals knows the requirements of each bank. Ask that person to bring it to your attention immediately if the package is incomplete for any reason.

> If anything goes bad, I did it.
> If anything goes semi-good, then we did it.
> If anything goes real good, then you did it.
> That's all it takes to get people to win football games.
>
> - Paul 'Bear' Bryant

## The Service Department

Coordination with the service manager is very important, particularly in the area of accessory sales. You must persuade him or her that you plan on selling all kinds of accessories. Ideally, your cost on these accessories should not be any higher than cost to the parts department, although this is virtually never the case. If there is a mark-up to you, first of all, you should be aware of that. Know what the parts department costs are. Secondly, the mark-up should be reasonable. since you should sell the same products for the same price they are offered by Parts, you should have the opportunity to make some money. If you help the service manager with parts sales, the service manager will help you by arranging timely detailing, coordinating sub-let appointments and by encouraging the service advisors to present service contracts.

Work with the service manager to quickly resolve any problems with service contract claims. The service drive is a great source of service contract business. As always, communication is important. Keep service advisors up to date on programs and prices.

When you sell accessories that require application or installation by the service department, make sure they get copies of Due Bills or Get Readies. They should have them on file, so that they are prepared for the customer who calls to make an appointment or who expects the work to be done at the first service. Give the parts department a copy, so they can ensure the products are in stock.

Keep a file in your office with the names of contact people for every service contract company with whom your dealership has done business. You need to be prepared to assist the service manager in verifying contracts or coverages for previous customers who come in with claims.

Check with the service contract company marketing representative to clarify the policy on service drive sales. Some companies allow used car service contracts to be sold in the drive, some don't. If you are helping the service manager, and you are making it worthwhile for the service advisors, the service department can assist with follow-up service contract sales.

- Offer sales incentives to service advisors

- Update service advisors on programs and prices

- Offer incentives to the cashier for service contract sales.

- For sub-let business, be responsible for coordination with Service.

- Deliver timely copies of Due Bills and Get Readies to Service.

- Keep a current list of accessories available through the parts department, with cost and retail prices. Be sure that retail prices are the same across departments.

- Deliver copies of Due Bills to Parts, so supplies not in stock can be ordered.

- Establish a service contract follow-up system, using names from customer Repair Orders. Contact customers who are approaching the deadline for qualifying for new car coverage.. Remind them of what a good deal it is and offer an incentive for responding.

- Keep copies of all the previous service contract programs used by your dealership. You never know when questions will arise as to coverages and promises made in the past. Also, keep transfer and cancellation forms from previous administrators. If you don't have any, find some generic forms (See Service Contract chapter).

> Money is of no value;
> it cannot spend itself.
> All depends on the skill
> of the spender.
>
> - Ralph Waldo Emerson

## The Dealer Principal

When you are not sure what 'policy' is about a particular matter, ask the dealer and get it from the source. After all, you are his or her representative. Will he 'recourse' paper? Does he want 'market price' for service contracts? Or the same price every time? Should credit applications be complete before they reach the finance office? How important does he or she consider a current registration on the trade? Is the F&I office expected to close every deal? Who makes the ultimate decision to roll a car? If you don't have the owner's support in matters like these, there is little point in trying to enforce them yourself. No one will take you seriously.

Does the sales desk participate in the F&I reserve? Successful dealers are fully in support of profit, wherever it can be found. The desk will sell more cars and make more money if they can take a cheaper deal on the front to make more money on the back. Can you 'spiff' salespeople for assistance above and beyond the call of duty? Can you run a contest every now and then?

When you want to initiate or expand a program, talk to the dealer and get your support there first. Should we put a dealership-wide effort into expanding leasing? Should we start selling service contracts in the service drive? Only the most provincial dealers still work one department against the other. The smart owners recognize that everybody benefits when the departments are working together.

You are expected to make the judgement calls in order to 'spot' deliver cars. Know what the dealer's philosophy is here. Is he conservative? How much risk does she want to take? Good communication in this relationship will give you the confidence to help the store put more cars in the street. You must know that your approach has the dealer's support. You need to know that the dealer realizes that she is not just in the car business, but also the finance, insurance and aftermarket business. Even in a small dealership, F&I can contribute significantly to the bottom line.

## Note on Notes

> Every man takes the limits of his own field of vision for the limits of the world.
>
> - Schopenhauer

❖ Write notes about everything. When did you submit the deal? What were the stipulations, if any, on the approval? If you heard no stipulations, confirm that ... and write "As is" or "No Stips.".

❖ How much does the proof of income need to support?

❖ What was the reason for the customer's ninth bankruptcy?

❖ Don't rely on memory. Write it down. Put a date on all your notes.

❖ So much of the car business is based on verbal agreement. In order to hold someone to their word, you need to have accurate notes. The credit buyer keeps meticulous notes, you can be sure. If he or she can recall what was said during a particular conversation, and you can't, the lender has the advantage.

❖ Notes should be kept in the deal with all the other paperwork. Something may come up two years down the road, and you will need to be able to reconstruct a deal ... and the reasons for taking the action you did. Notes on the front of a deal help as the deal is being worked. Other managers and salespeople are able to check on the status of a deal if you can't be reached.

❖ Keep a yellow legal pad on your desk. Make a list in the morning of things to do that day. As you do them, cross them off the list. In the course of a day, you will have numerous telephone conversations. You will make commitments to do certain things, which you will undoubtedly forget if you don't write them down. Each time you commit to do something, and then forget, your credibility suffers.

❖ This is the first piece of advice given by experienced F&I managers to rookies. Don't rely on your memory. Write it down.

> As I grow older,
> I pay less attention
> to what men say.
> I just watch what they do.
>
> - Andrew Carnegie

## The Finance Office

Your image and the appearance of your office should engage your customer and establish the context of their experience. It is the office of a professional manager ... someone with authority. This context - your appearance and manner, the way you keep the office you work in - determine the expectations of the customer. A successful image is confident, competent and consistent. Look around your office. Any contradictions to the rule will weaken the effect of your image.

It is a fact that the 500 most commonly used words in the English language have over 14,000 different meanings. Your strong image will directly influence which meanings your customer chooses.

Don't spit in the wastebasket, at least while the customer is looking. Remove the coffee cups. put away the newspaper, dust your monitor screen and so on. Eating in the office ... and leaving the room smelling like the Taco Pit is probably one of the most common mistakes ... since we all get so busy. Sit in the customer's chair and look around your office. Would you trust what you see?

It is a feature of the human brain that it assembles meaning by testing for contradiction. This is how the brain forms reliable plans. In fact, the right brain of an apprehensive customer will be putting out a steady signal, looking for a contradiction to your professional image. Finding no contradiction, he or she will be much more inclined to believe what you say. (This is true for each of us in our personal lives as well, by the way. Contradiction of personal values has been shown to lead to low self-esteem and ill-health. The word 'health' means 'wholeness').

You can literally create the experience of the customer. You can influence his or her assumptions about the world, if you do your job well. You are the only manager that the customer if likely to meet. Your signature will authorize the sale. You should look and sound like the professional you are. F&I managers should wear business suits and always look professional. Shoes should always be shined. Hands are important. Invest in yourself.

> People's minds are changed through observation and not through argument.
>
> - Will Rogers

- ❖ Dress conservatively, like a banker.
- ❖ Have a clean desk with only the current deal visible.
- ❖ Don't have any piles in your office. Piles mean unfinished work.
- ❖ Add a plant or two.
- ❖ A family picture adds a nice touch.
- ❖ Make all forms easily accessible.
- ❖ Don't have labels stuck to equipment with phone numbers, etc.
- ❖ Always have a notepad handy.
- ❖ Keep a sales tax by county list available.
- ❖ Minimize distractions. Draw curtains over glass walls. Face customers away from windows.
- ❖ Keep a binder listing accessories, with wholesale and retail cost.
- ❖ Subscribe to a monthly book of credit union rates and programs.
- ❖ Keep a business card file of all the cards you come across.
- ❖ Keep a telephone book of all the numbers you may ever need, including service and support numbers for all systems. Update the book with new and potential contacts.
- ❖ Keep a binder of finance and lease rates. The book should be organized in such a way that it is easy for other managers to use.
- ❖ Keep a log book. List each deal by Report of Sale number as it leaves your office. Include stock number, date, customer, trade, salesperson, reserve, service contract gross, accessories, total deal, accumulated total and method of payment (source of funding).

> You must have a good time meeting people,
> if you expect them to have a good time meeting you.
>
> - Dale Carnegie

## The Deal

It should be the stated policy of the dealership to treat every deal as a potential finance or lease deal. If a customer insists on obtaining his or her own financing, a customer application should still be completed and a 'cashable' contract should be signed. Except in the most dire circumstances, a customer should not be handed a purchase order and sent off to his own bank. Even on a deal that is strictly cash, a five-line statement should be taken and a credit profile run.

It is helpful to the process if checks are not written, nor final rates or creditworthiness decided, until the customer is in F&I. The salesperson ought not to enter into a discussion of finance terms beyond the basics. A common mistake is to close a customer on lease terms for example, only later to discover that the customer is not lease-worthy. By providing bottom-line rates and terms before the customer has agreed to buy the car is at best prolonging the negotiation and is perhaps an invitation to shop.

Be prepared to close a finance deal on the spot. Evaluate the credit profile. Calculate the debt ratio. Learn how to read financial statements and tax returns. Know what your competition is offering. Save your customer the time and trouble of shopping around. You have a valuable service to offer and you deserve fair compensation for your services on the customer's behalf.

Establish your role as an executive at the beginning of your meeting with the customer. Ask for any information that maybe missing from the credit application, like other car loans. How will they verify income?

Disclose the contract completely the same way every time. Point to each figure on the contract with your pen. Explain "This is the price of the car ... this is the sales tax "...etc. There is no need to say the figures out loud. Knowing that you always disclose the information the same way will protect you against the customer who might return six months later and claim she was never told the proice of the car.

> A man without a smiling face ought not to open a shop.
>
> - Chinese proverb

- ❖ Once the deal is made, make sure you have all the relevant paperwork before you meet the customer: cap sheet from the sales desk, worksheet, credit statement, credit profile, current registration and trade appraisal, proof of insurance, title or exact payoff and a copy of the driver's license.

- ❖ Load the deal in the computer and print out the initial paperwork - registration, odometer statement, insurance and trade paperwork. You want to avoid a situation where the customer is sitting, watching you do all this while she is wondering what is going to happen to her next.

- ❖ Examine the trade paperwork. Is the person who is here to sign everything actually the registered owner? Is there a lien? Do you have the correct mileage? Will there be any fees due?

- ❖ Communicate with the salesperson. How is the customer planning to pay for the car? What are their plans for its use?

- ❖ Look at the customer statement from a sales point of view. Is the customer someone who travels and puts high miles on the vehicle? This would shorten the factory warranty. Is he an older customer who would benefit from "guaranteed" credit insurance?

- ❖ Encourage a proper introduction by the salesperson. Be introduced as "The Business Manager" ... not "the guy who does the paperwork...."

- ❖ If the registration shows a lien and the customer claims the loan is paid off, he should sign a statement of facts indicating "no liens or encumbrances".

- ❖ When a customer makes any kind of cash payment, give her a separate receipt. A copy of the receipt stays in the book.

- ❖ It is important to complete the customer statement and the credit profile as early in the course of working a deal as possible. Will the customer qualify for a lease or extended terms? Will you need a 75% downpayment? Do you need to switch to a more suitable car? Will you need a cap reduction on the lease? Your communication here may be essential to making the deal.

> The quality of a person's life is in direct proportion to their commitment to excellence, regardless of their chosen field of endeavor.
>
> - Vince Lombardi

## Follow Up

Follow up is the administrative aspect of the F&I responsibilities which, when done well, usually goes unrecognized. But when it's not done well, it's a constant source of aggravation. The key here is prevention. Do as much work as possible in terms of income verification, insurance confirmation, and so on ... meeting the stipulations *before* the car is delivered. Work to obtain 'as-is' approvals whenever possible. After delivery, it is legend in the car business that there is less urgency in the customer's need to cooperate. A buyer who has changed his or her mind may never provide the documentation you require ... aware that the dealer will not be funded and hoping you will take the car back instead.

## One Pay

If a wayward customer, even after all your reasoned persuasions, insists on obtaining her own financing, note the source of the loan and the loan officer's name and number. Be sure that you have the signatures on the paperwork necessary to finance the car yourself, if the need arises. Call the customer the next day and offer to assist in any way. Remind her of the option you have provided. Follow up again in three days.

## Income Verification

Negotiate with your source for an 'as-is' approval whenever possible. If you can, submit income verification with the application. If you know you are going to need it, ask the salesperson to get documentation up front, or ask the customer to bring it at the time of delivery. Unprofessional salespeople who avoid the issue of income verification can become the victim of a remorseful and suddenly uncooperative buyer. If you don't have the required verification before delivery, arrange for the documentation to be provided in the quickest way possible.
Be sure to have verified the information verbally: "What do you show as your adjusted gross income on the front page of last year's tax return?"

Every finance manager has encountered the challenge of financing a customer who has quoted the gross income to his business as his own personal income. Don't avoid these clarifications and hope you'll never have to face the problem. Who else will have to solve it? Have the customer sign a document agreeing to provide the stipulated documentation and state in writing how much income will be verified. Call the customer the next day to remind him. This is another reason for getting the daily list of receivables.

> We will either find a way or make one.
>
> - Hannibal

### Insurance Verification

Put as much information as possible on the Agreement to Furnish Insurance form. Always obtain the company, as well as the name and number of the agent. If the customer delays adding the vehicle to her insurance policy, funding will be delayed as well. During the delivery, emphasize that, though there may be a grace period, the agent should be notified right away. Give the customer a card showing the lienholder information and a contact at the bank. Before insurance is verified, the dealer is particularly exposed if the vehicle is delivered on a lease. 'Automatic' 30-day extension on a common minimum policy is not even close to the $100,000/$300,000 coverage required on a lease. The dealership may be liable until the deal is funded.

When you know that a bank has received the contract package, call the funding department. Make a point of getting acquainted with the person at the bank who processes your deals. Ask if your deal has gone through for funding, or if there's anything you can do to assist. As a rule, you should know that your deal has been funded (because of the excellence of your communication with the bank) before the check arrives.

### Make it Routine

Unless you are one of the fortunate few to have an assistant to take care of this kind of work, make it easy on yourself. Take the first hour in the morning, or the hour before lunch ... or whatever hour suits you best. Make it the same hour every day. Don't second guess yourself. For example, "That customer was a good guy ... I just know he'll come through." He may have been busy. Call everybody and leave a message at the very least.

### Telephone Manners

When you leave a message, include a word or two about why you called. Since so much of the car business is conducted over the phone, proper manners are critical. Always return call promptly. At the beginning of a call that you initiate, always ask, "Did I get you at a bad time?" Enlist the other person's attention. If the person is distracted, it may be better to call back later. It's cliche, but it works ... smile on the telephone. Use your voice deliberately. Vary your inflection and timing. Let your voice carry your purpose. It is an intimate medium. Use it that way. An *enthusiastic* voice ... not a loud voice ... is a welcome encounter in the course of a long business day.

> A winner is someooone who recognizes his God-given talents, works his tail off to develop them into skills, and uses these skills to accomplish his goals.
>
> - Larry Bird

## Forecasting

Some companies require annual or even monthly forecasting and others require no forecasting at all. Whether or not you are required to do so, you certainly should consider trends and prepare for the future. Of course, the profitability of the F&I department is directly related to the production of the sales department. The key element in judging F&I production is the average profit per retail unit (P.R.U.). In order to forecast successfully, start by looking at the past year. ask questions like:

What % of last year's deals were financed?
What % were leased?
What was the % of service contract penetration?
What was the average reserve for the deals that were financed?
What was the average reserve per lease?
What was the average service contract profit?
Which accessories produced the most income?
What % of total income was each product/service?
Are there discernable trends?
What was last year's P.R.U.?

Then you might look to the future:

What has changed from last year to this?
Are vehicles more expensive?
What is the economic environment?
Is there a direction to the market as a whole?
Are people keeping their cars longer than before?
Which way are interest rates going?
How are gas prices?
Any regulation changes?

Much of your forecast will depend on what the sales department has to say, but you should be looking at how people will be paying for those cars. If people have been keeping cars longer, they will be more likely to appreciate the value of a service contract. If rates are headed up, now is a good time to buy.

> Prediction is very difficult, especially about the future.
>
> - Neils Bohr
> Nobel Laureate in Physics

Look at changes you plan to make internally:
Will you add an assistant to take care of follow up?
Are there new and accommodating funding sources on the horizon?
What new programs will current sources offer?
Are factory warranties changing?
Can you expand service contract sales to the service drive?
Will a change in the way deals are worked benefit F&I?
Is it time for a contest or a 'spiff' program?

How will all these factors affect the percentage of penetration and the average per sale? Each increase in forecast figures must be accompanied by an expanation and a plan. Any decrease in figures should be explained as an act of God. Usually increases are produced by a combination of elements ... increased penetration percentages and either lower costs or higher prices. Remember, although it is true that "gross is only a state of mind", dealer principals appreciate realistic scenarios and do not take dreamers seriously.

A very basic forecast for a store that intends to sell 1000 vehicles might look like this:

| 1991 | # | % | $ per unit | Gross |
|---|---|---|---|---|
| Contracts | 500 | 50% | 900 | 450,000 |
| Leases | 175 | 17.5% | 1200 | 210,000 |
| Service Contracts | 600 | 60% | 400 | 240,000 |
| LA&H | 150 | 15% | 200 | 30,000 |
| After Market | | | | |
| **TOTAL** | 1000 | PRU | 930 | 930,000 |

When looked at from this perspective, it is easy to see what steps to take in order to increase PRU. For example, adding accessory sales would put the average over $1000. The purpose of forecasting, besides the need to establish a budget, is to require a manager to think about his or her market and develop a plan. Be ready to defend your numbers on every line.

> If you don't know
> where you're going,
> any path will take you there.
>
> - Sioux proverb

## Setting Goals

Goals are absolutely essential. Even if you are not required to submit a forecast, you should take the time and trouble to set some goals with specific deadlines. Daily attention to your goals keeps you focussed and alert to opportunity. Goals must have four characteristics:

**A goal must be specific:** "I want to make more money" becomes "I want to increase the gross income to this department by 10% by the end of the first quarter."

**A goal must be measurable:** "I don't want to miss an opportuntiy" becomes "I will ask *every* customer for the sale."

**A goal must be realistic:** "I want to make more money than God" becomes "I want to raise my PRU by $100 a car in three months."

**A goal must be relevant:** "I want to learn how to reprogram the mainframe" becomes "I want to be able to perform every F&I function available in the system without referring to the manual."

**Well-planned goals can and should be broken down into smaller parts:**

Increasing the gross income by 10% becomes:
    increasing service contract penetration by 5%
    plus increasing average finance reserve by $50 a car
    plus increasing lease penetration by 3 leases a month.

Using goals to navigate in this way, you should have a good idea where you stand in relation to your objectives on any day of the month. If you are a little ahead of goals that have been carefully set, then you should enjoy a sense of accomplishment. If you are a little behind, then you know that extra effort is called for. Your goals (or plans) actually determine how you perceive information. You do have goals, whether you admit to them or not. Be in control of this process. Choose your goals carefully. Expect to get those things that will make you happy. Be prepared to work very hard for them ... and you just can't lose.

> It's what you learn after you know it all that counts.
>
> - John Wooden

- ❖ Given all the laws that must be followed regarding compliance and disclosure, it is very important that the F&I manager be professional. What is said in front of the customer, even casually, may be construed as an *implied warranty* in court.

- ❖ Include an article on financing or leasing in the dealership newsletter. Have monthly article and/or special.

- ❖ Any time that a question arises that you can't answer, find out what the answer is. A professional never stops learning. This is the only way to become an expert.

- ❖ Don't procrastinate. Those less-than-pleasant tasks will never go away. They will just ruin your day if you don't take care of them.

- ❖ Return phone calls promptly.

- ❖ Be sure you know how the reserve is paid by each lender. Which banks pay a percentage up front, which pay as earned, what the chargeback policies are.

- ❖ Check the reserves against your log as they come in. Ask the office to make you aware of any differences between what you set up and what was actually paid.

- ❖ Create an evidence manual. Clip out articles relative to financing and leasing. Include tables showing current T bill rates, loan rates and so on. Keep the book current ... "only yesterday, in the Anytown Times, there was this article about the benefits of leasing ...".

# Notes

# Notes

# Forms

Life's nothing but paperwork.

- Gustav Mahler

## Take care with the fundamentals.

Doing routine paperwork, or rather, the failure to do routine paperwork properly, is often an unnecessary source of problems. Precisely because it is so routine, developing correct habits is important. Handling the legal aspects of a car sale efficiently and professionally establishes the credibility of the finance manager. He or she clearly appears to be someone who knows exactly what they are doing.

Dealing with this part of the job correctly also enhances the relationship between the finance and the business offices. The significance of this relationship is not to be overlooked. Too often, this relationship is not what it could be because the staff responsible for processing the DMV and the contracts feel that F&I doesn't care about the finer points of the paperwork. In the worst cases, this relationship even becomes adversarial rsther than cooperative. This is a mistake. Those who work in the business office will help you ... and look out for your best interest ... if you do what you can to help them. Efficient handling of the daily paperwork is a major step in the right direction.

## About Signing Forms

Paperwork should be signed at the dealership whenever possible. Sometimes, of course, it will be necessary to take contracts to the customer ... you must always do whatever it takes. Emphasize to the salesperson that business is best done in the building. This is obviously the only way you will have an opportuntiy to make your presentation ... and the three-day recission period (as in real estate) may apply if the customer signs at home or at the office.

Develop the habit of leading a customer through the process the same way every time. This way, the procedure occupies less of your thought process and you are less likely to make a mistake. Gradually the forms will automatically cue the legal details that you need to check for ... and for the trial closes of your various presentations. For example, noticing high mileage on a trade, you may comment on the amount of driving the customer does. You might note that he or she might be out of factory warranty in half the usual time. They may want to consider a service contract.

The basic forms are similar from state to state. The California forms from 1991 are used here.

> Three people were at work on a contruction site. All were doing the same job, but when each was asked what his job was, the answers varied.
>
> "Breaking rocks", the first replied. "Earning my living", the second said. "Helping to build a cathedral", said the third.
>
> - Peter Schultze
> CEO Porsche

- ❖ If you need more information on the customer statement, do it before you begin signing the routine forms.

- ❖ Always have a pen available for each person who has to sign.

- ❖ Do not mark signature fields beforehand with a marker pen. Perhaps it is a subtle thing, but by marking the place with a pen in front of the customer, you are exhibiting authority and control.

- ❖ Get in the habit of disclosing the forms the same way every time.

- ❖ Be positive and enthusiastic. Create an atmosphere where it's ok for the customer to be excited about their new car.

- ❖ Use the time while completing the routine paperwork to make conversation. Talk about where the customer lives or about their job. "I see you live in San Francisco. How do you like living in the city?" "So you're from back East, how do you like California?"

- ❖ If you are facing two customers, be sure to address both equally. One of them may take your side in the presentation.

- ❖ Once a form is signed, move it to the side, out of reach.

- ❖ Have an envelope or folder handy for the customer's copies.

- ❖ After beginning the routine paperwork, begin your presentation from something that has come up in the conversation. "You had your last car for quite a while, will you be keeping the new car as long?" "What about using that credit union loan to consolidate those debts we talked about? The signature loan would be a lower rate than the credit cards and the lower debt ratio will earn you a preferred rate at our bank."

- ❖ Set the temporary registration where the salesperson can pick it up when she comes to collect her customer.

# Power of Attorney

"Your signature on this form allows me to register your new car on your behalf."

| POWER OF ATTORNEY VEHICLE/VESSEL | VEHICLE LICENSE NO. OR VESSEL CF NO. New |
|---|---|
| VEHICLE OR HULL IDENTIFICATION NO. WDBCA123456789101 | MAKE OF VEHICLE OR VESSEL BUILDER MBZ |

To the Department of Motor Vehicles, Sacramento, Calif., and to whom it may concern:

I (print full name) Customer   John   A.
             LAST      FIRST    MIDDLE

I (print full name) Customer   Mary   T.
             LAST      FIRST    MIDDLE

the undersigned do hereby duly appoint the following named person or company,

Everyday Motors

to act as my/our attorney in fact, to sign papers and documents that may be necessary in order to secure California registration of or to transfer my/our interest in the above described vehicle or vessel.

I/We further agree to guarantee and save the State of California and the Director of Motor Vehicles from all responsibility which might accrue from the issuance of California registration or transfer of such vehicle or vessel.

Note: An attorney in fact cannot make an affidavit or certificate of the truth of facts unknown to him.

| SIGNED X | DAYTIME TELEPHONE NUMBER ( ) 408 456-1111 |
|---|---|
| SIGNED X | DATE (MONTH & YEAR) August 31, 1991 |

NO. 146 REG. 260 (REV. 4/88) LAW PRINTING CO., INC.   CALL (800) 422-3102

**Two Powers of Attorney are needed on every retail deal except leases.**

❖ Signatures should match the name as spelled out on the Report of Sale exactly, including the middle initial or the middle name.

❖ Primary Buyer signs first.

❖ Have the cusomter sign two powers of attorney, at least one of them blank. The second may be used as a back-up in the file or for trade-in titlework, since the vehicle information doesn't always print through the 9-pack. There are several other circumstances for which a blank power of attorney would expedite business for your DMV secretary.

# Odometer Statement

"With this form I am telling you that the miles on your new car are true and that we did not change them.

I need you to acknowledge that I told you that."

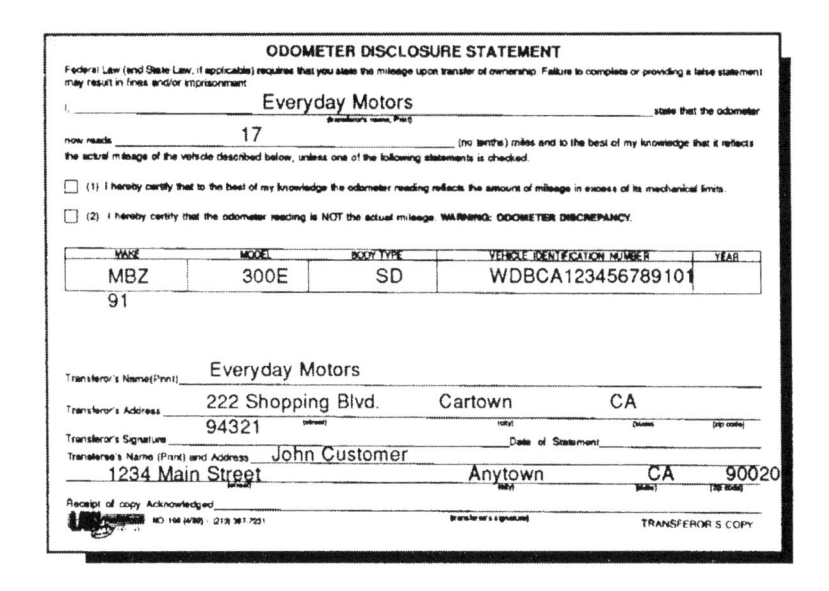

**An odometer statement is required on every deal, including leases and deals that are "Hold for Resale".**

- ❖ Be sure that the mileage is taken from the car. Remember that it is your signature that verifies the accuracy of the odometer.

- ❖ Know what the two boxes available on the form mean, in case you are asked.

- ❖ The customer is not agreeing that the stated mileage is actually true (How would they know?). The customer is only acknowledging your statement.

- ❖ Set aside a customer copy.

# Report of Sale

Write in "For Resale" if that applies

Be sure the I.D. # prints legibly

# axles needed on commercial vehicles only

Use 'County' as a reminder to check the tax rate

In California you must use a street address, not a P.O. Box

Add 'Lienholder' after money is in.

Be sure the signature matches the printed name exactly. Signatures may be added on behalf of the customer, with power of attorney.

Retail selling price, including accessories (no tax, license or finance charges)

Write in "For Resale" if that applies

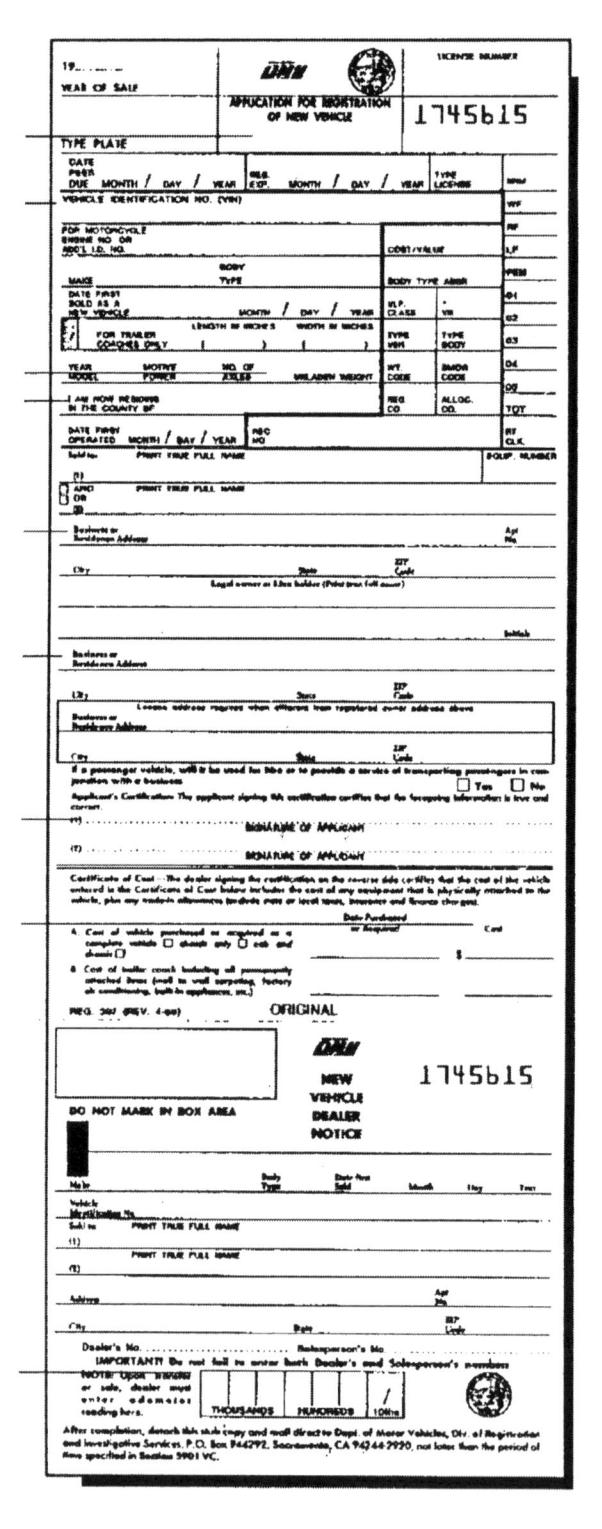

- ❖ Use the Reports of Sale in their numbered sequence.

- ❖ Reports of Sale are the property of the DMV in California and must be surrendered if not used.

- ❖ The 'Dealer Notice' must be sent in within 5 days. These conditions mean 'don't trip a car until you are putting it in the street'. There is potential liability on the part of the dealer for an accident caused by a new owner, if the 5-day notice is not submitted on time.

- ❖ In California, the temporary registration is good for 90 days.

- ❖ Abbreviate automobile makes to 5 letters: TYOTA, CELCA ...

- ❖ Abbreviate body type: SD, CP, PU, WG ...

- ❖ For used cars, show O/S for cars not previously registered in the state.

- ❖ Check with the DMV secretary to see if he or she marks the 'or' option automatically whenever there are two people on the registration.

- ❖ In case a mistake was made, or the car was not delivered, write "VOID" across the form and give all copies to the DMV secretary.

- ❖ It is good policy, whenever possible, only to add a Legal Owner to a Report of Sale after you have been paid in full.

- ❖ When you are selling a car "For Resale", the broker (non-franchised dealer) will require the top copy of the Report of Sale, in order to submit it with his own USed Car R/S. This establishes a 'chain of ownership'. Keep a copy in the file, along with a copy of the broker's retail license and a resale card with his resale number. Release the top copy only after the deal is funded.

---

*If you put a mouse into a maze and it gets it right the first time, it has not learned to run the maze. It does not learn until it makes some mistakes and learns to avoid them.*

- Jacob Bronowski

# Agreement to Furnish Insurance

"With whom do you have insurance now?"

What is your agent's name?

Where is she or he located?

What is their phone number?"

**The Agreement to Furnish Insurance is needed on every retail deal. For leases, there may be a section on the lease form itself.**

❖ It is important to verify current insurance: liability and comprehensive/collision.

❖ Many dealers require a copy of the driver's insurance card as standard procedure.

❖ If the customer does not have insurance, sell it to him. At least provide a temporary binder. Or call an agent to bind him. (Always have the contact information of one or two helpful agents.)

❖ Note that the form indicates that the seller may obtain insurance and the buyer agrees to pay for it.

❖ The form also indicates that the buyer assumes liability for damage and any claims against the vehicle.

❖ The lending source will delay funding until insurance coverage is confirmed ... by using only information that you provide. Include the agent's phone number, even if you have to get it yourself.

❖ If the customer is leasing, be sure the amount of coverage is appropriate.

# Notice to Co-Signer

"On this form you are both acknowledging that the co-signer is equally responsible for the debt."

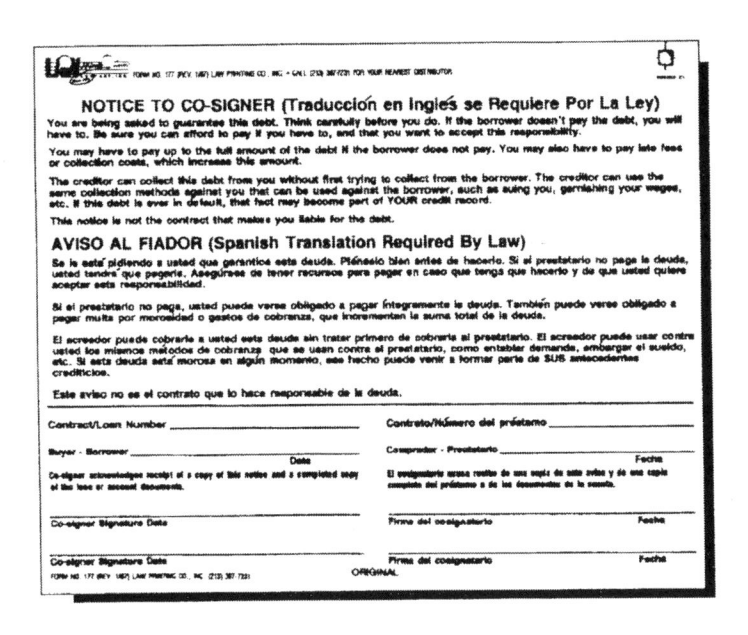

**This form is needed every time the second party to a contract is not the spouse or a company guarantor.**

- ❖ Usually, only close relatives are considered to be eligible for co-signing, but exceptions can be made on an individual basis.

- ❖ Usually a co-signer is not considered to be a possibility for a lease, but this policy may vary according to the leasing source.

- ❖ Co-signer are generally considered to be support for lack of suitable credit history, sometimes as support for bad credit and not usually as support for the primary buyer's lack of sufficient monthly income.

- ❖ A co-signed contract is a good opportunity for a credit insurance sale.

# 9 Pack

"Here you are telling me that the miles on the car you are trading in are true and that you didn't change them".

1. "And this is a bill of sale on your trade".

2. "And here you are authorizing me to pay off your car".

3. "Here we are agreeing that if the payoff is more than you estimated, you will pay us the difference, and if it less, we will pay you.

4. "And these are powers of attorney so that I can change the registration on your trade".

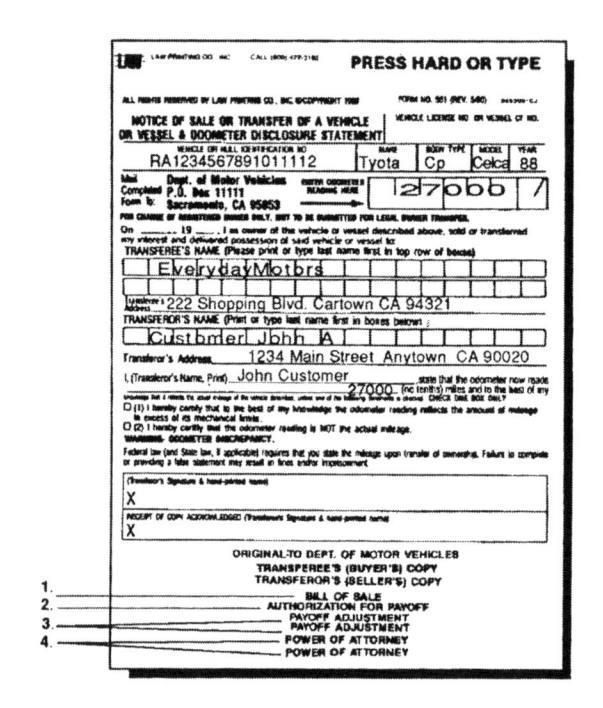

**A 9-pack is needed with every trade-in vehicle.**

1. Always see a current registration and check the driver's license to verify that the person signing the bill of sale is entitled to do so.

2. Check for a lienholder. If a lien shows on the registration, always obtain the title; or a request for a duplicate title with a Statement of Facts that there is no lien.

3. If the registration is in two names and is not marked "or", be sure that both owners sign. Note: in California "/" indicates "and".

4. Vehicles that are registered in a company name must be signed off in that name, with an authorized signature.

5. If the trade is a leased vehicle, the customer must sign an "Odometer Statement for a Leased Vehicle".

6. If you wish to emphasize that the payoff is the customer's estimate, ask him or her to write in the figure when signing the payoff adjustment form.

# Payoff Verification

Get the mailing address for the payoff bank

Telephone number is important

Account number is important

If you are financing the new car with the same source, is there a re-lease figure?

Allow 10 days for processing

Always get the name of the person quoting the payoff

Payoff should always be verified by F&I.

**PAY OFF VERIFICATION**

Customer's Name: Customer
Address: 
Car Financed By: Friendly Finance
Address: 1800 Lendabuck Way, Zillions OH 45345
Phone: 
Acct. No. 123-23-7890-21  Date Opened:
Hi Balance:
Terms:
Balance:  Date Last Paid:  Next Due:
Rebate:
Net Pay Off: 1200.00          1200.00
Security:
Good Until: 9-7-91
How Paid:
Spoke To: Fred
Verified By: Dave
Date: 8-30-91   Time:

**A payoff should be verified by the Business Manager on every trade with a lien. Whenever possible, the payoff should be verified before the deal is worked.**

- Ask for a payoff figure that is good for at least 10 days.

- If there is a daily interest accrual, calculate the payoff for 10 days.

- The account number is often found in the customer's credit profile.

- Establish a procedure for collecting payoff differences. Call the customer immediately and mail an invoice the same day. Offer to help the customer by adjusting the payoff figure on the original contract, if that would be useful.

- Return payoff refunds after the deal has been funded.

# Leased Trade-in Odometer Statement

**This form is required on every trade-in that is a leased vehicle.**

- ❖ The lessee (customer) is certifying to the lessor (bank) that the current mileage on the car is true.

- ❖ The lessee signs on the "Lessee's Signature" line.

- ❖ This form must be completed and sent to the bank along with the Authorization for Payoff.

- ❖ This form should be signed at the same time as the 9 pack.

- ❖ The lienholder on the trade will not release title without this form.

> It isn't what you have or who you are or where you are or what you are doing that makes you happy or unhappy. It is what you think about it.
>
> - Dale Carnegie

These are the forms most commonly used for a standard deal. DMV forms vary of course, from state to state, but most of the deal forms and procedures are common around the country.

This part of the daily responsibilites of the business manager are routine. You should approach this aspect of the process the same way every time. This way the procedure becomes a habit and you are much less likely to forget the little things - like checking the registration of the trade, the odometer statement on a lease, the spouse signing the 'Authorization for payoff" when the registration reads "and". Doing these things the same way every time also allows your mind some freedom to concentrate on those aspects of the deal that require your close attention, calling on your creativity and highest professional skills.

The real work begins with the Customer Statement.

# Notes

# Notes

# The Customer Statement

*Patience is a most necessary quality for business: many a man would rather you heard his story than grant his request.*

*- Earl of Chesterfield*

**Most finance institutions now use computerized scoring systems to evaluate applications.** Information is entered directly from the form into a database by a data-entry clerk and then scored according to pre-determined criteria by a computer. The score is affected by factors like the number of personal references, whether the customer shows a savings account, how long the customer has been in the same line of work ... and so on. Not too long ago, points were awarded for having a home phone. Important to note here is that before the credit analyst even sees your deal, his or her perception of it will be influenced by the quantity and quality of the information provided on the application.

**An application that is neat and complete has a positive effect on the buyer.** A messy form has a negative effect. First impressions *do* make a difference. Do not underestimate this effect. You are constantly working to impress your buyer with how much you care about getting your deals bought. Make sure that salespeople take applications in a way that works for you. That is why you are a manager.

**The customer statement is the business manager's opportuntity to provide additional helpful information to the bank**: a car loan through a credit union that doesn't appear in the credit profile; an additional source of income; a large amount of money on deposit or invested; continuous employment in the same line of work.

**The credit statement is the only image the bank will see of your customer over which you have any influence.** When the buyer is considering your customer, he or she is picturing the application you submitted. Make that work for you. It is the chance to build two of the four 'C's of credit worthiness: Character and Capacity (ability to pay). The other two, Credit-ability and Collateral, are discussed later. Use the opportunity to show your customer in the best possible light.

**The business manager should be involved in every deal from the beginning.** The importance of taking the customer statement as early as possible cannot be overemphasized. The information that you gather at this point, including the credit profile, will often determine how you structure the deal. this will not be true in every case of course. The majority of your sales will be to very qualified buyers. However, the sales you may lose because you didn't structure the deal appropriately from the outset will sometimes make the difference between a good month and a great month.

> Things may come to those who wait, but only the things left by those who hustle.
>
> - Abraham Lincoln

It is much more difficult to switch a customer from a lease to a purchase after a lower lease payment has been quoted. A cap reduction is much harder to get after a customer has been quoted little or nothing down. These difficulties are compounded by the proliferation of 'special programs'. A customer who is locked into a special factory-subsidized rate may take personal offense at being refused the 'special' deal.

In the marginal cases, knowing which program will have the best chance of being bought at the bank is crucial. In fact, knowing which bank you will go to may determine the whole structure of your interview with the customer, since you can anticipate the particular information the bank will be looking for ... for example, smaller, local banks put more weight on stability, etc....

Equally important to resolve early is the husband-wife situation. Sometimes a spouse will want to put the car only in his or her name. According to the Equal Opportunity Credit Act, each spouse is entitled to be considered without regard to marital status. However, you might need the income or the credit from the other partner to strengthen the deal. Resolving this as early as possible in the process allows the deal to build successfully, rather than having to be repaired later.

In all these situations, your motivation is the same as the customer's. You want the process to move forward as smotthly as possible. You want the experience of buying a car to be a pleasant one and you want to satisfy the customer's needs. Working from this point of view, you are truly offering a service. A service for which you deserve to be paid. A service for which the customer will gladly pay you accordingly.

## Calculating a Debt Ratio

Look at income from two different points of view: as much as possible coming in and as little as possible going out.

| Income | Outgo |
|---|---|
| Regular monthly salary | Shared mortgage payment |
| Commission | Shared rent |
| Bonus | Co-signed loan |
| Spousal income | Balances recently paid |
| Rental income | Divorce settlement |
| Dividends and Interest | Allocate accounts to ex-spouse |
| Child support | |
| Car allowance | |
| Depreciation | |

Look carefully at the dates when checking debt balances on the credit profile. Make sure you are only dealing with *current* debt. Reduce the debt ratio by raising income and eliminating debt. Document your case.

Your credibility with the bank is strengthened if it is obvious to the credit buyer that you look at your deals critically and carefully. It is to your advantage to anticipate, and prepare for, challenges to the deal. One of the most common challenges is the debt ratio. This is another reason for getting involved in the deal at an early stage. By making the observation to the sales desk that the customer may be trying to buy a car that the bank will consider too much for him or her, it might be possible to have the salesperson guide the customer to a less expensive alternative.

If we all lived within our means, the car business would be the first to suffer. The responsibility falls on you to show the bank the customer can afford her dream machine. If you suspect that the debt ratio may become a problem, anticipate a solution by looking for extra income. Get a tax return and look for depreciation or Schedule C expenses, ask if any outstanding balances have been reduced, add the income of a spouse ....Learn to calulate a debt ratio and make it a practice to know how each of your sources looks at debt. Some don't like it at all, some will offset debt with equity, some will allow for a higher ratio if there's more discretionary income. Know your sources.

---

*Never ask of money spent*
*Where the spender thinks it went.*
*Nobody was ever meant*
*To remember or invent*
*What he did with every cent.*

*- Robert Frost*

> Facts do not cease to exist because they are ignored.
>
> - Aldous Huxley

The formula commonly used to calculate a debt ratio is
Gross Monthly Income x 75% = Net Monthly Income

House payment
+ Other car payment
+ 5% of each outstanding balance (from the credit profile)
+ the new car payment

= Total Monthly Outgo

Net Monthly Outgo Divided by Net Monthly Income = Debt Ratio

For example:
$5000 monthly gross x 75% = $3750 net monthly income

|   | |
|---|---|
|   | $750 house payment |
| + | $180 other car |
| + | $50 Visa ($1000 balance) |
| + | $25 Mastercard ($500 balance) |
| + | $275 new car |
| = | $1280 monthly outgo |

Debt Ratio = $1280 divided by $3750 = 34%

If this customer's house payment were $1500 a month, we would have a 54% debt ratio, which could be a problem. However, by talking to him, we discover that the Visa account is actually paid off and we can add back $8000 annual income which is listed as depreciation on his Schedule C. Now Outgo is $1980 and Income is $4417. Debt Ratio is now 45%

This debt ratio is still high, so we submit the deal to a bank that we know does not automatically add insurance expenses into the debt ratio. We point out to the bank that the customer has been on his job as a high school teacher for 20 years. He has 50% equity in his house, impeccable credit history and 30% downpayment. He has paid as agreed on a previous car loan with a similar balance. He stopped in to buy the car on his way to church, which besides going to work, is the only driving he ever does. By off-setting the higher debt ratio with other factors, namely the customer's character, collateral and credit-ability, we have a deal.

If the customer moved recently, was there a job-related reason?

Does the job description indicate responsibility?

Although the customer may have changed companies, is he still in the same line of work?

Does the income include bonuses? Car allowance? Up-coming raise?

What will last year's personal tax return show as Adjusted Gross Income?

Is the spouse employed? How much income can be documented?

If the customer is renting, does she own property elsewhere?

If he is paying a mortgage, what is the difference between the loan balance and the current market value of the property?

Are there any previous auto loans that are not shown in the credit profile?

Does the customer have a savings account as well as a checking account? Certificates of Deposit? Stocks and Bonds?

Personal references are important, especially on marginal applications.

Make sure it is signed.

# The Customer Statement

> We are what we repeatedly do.
>
> - Aristotle

- ❖ In the customer statement you are building the Character of the customer and her Capacity (ability to pay). Details count.

- ❖ Always have a complete customer statement for anything other than a straight cash deal. For a cash deal, get the first five lines verfied (name, address, birthdate, social security number and driver's license number).

- ❖ Train salespeople to take the application properly.

- ❖ Always include information on the spouse without a specific reason not to.

- ❖ CUSTOMER STATEMENTS SHOULD BE PRINTED IN BLOCK CAPITALS. Every word must be legible.

- ❖ Complete the application as early in the process as possible.

- ❖ Be sure every applicant signs the statement. Sources will not process the appication without a signature.

- ❖ Check the statement for completeness. Ask the salesperson immediately to obtain information that is incomplete.

- ❖ Complete enough residence information to cover a five-year history. Look for valid reasons for moving ... job transfer, raising a family, job offer ....

- ❖ Complete job history to cover five years. Connect changes in employment if possible.

- ❖ Add account numbers whever possible.

- ❖ Check relevant factors from the application against the credit profile: address, occupation, mortgage balance and auto loans, for example.

- ❖ Look for details that enhance the character and capacity of your customer: real estate equity, time in the same line of work, money in the bank, local references. Everything counts.

## Income Verification

There is no advantage to inflating monthly income on a credit statement. If the nature of the deal makes monthly income important, the bank will always stipulate verification. State income you can verify. Be thorough in your search for verification.

**Paycheck stub:** must have a year-to-date figure. Divide that figure by the number of weeks passed in the year leading up to the paycheck date. Count the weeks carefully. A common mistake is just to count months.

**Employment Contract:** if the customer is new on the job. A letter from the employer showing the job offer or stating date of hire, salary and benefits. Perhaps even a car allownce.

**Rental Agreement:** may justify high balances on the credit profile, as long as they show income greater than outgo. May not have been reported on the previous year's tax return.

**Copy of Divorce Settlement:** often can work both ways: prove court-ordered support and confirm that a particular debt is the responsibility of the ex-spouse.

**Personal Financial Statement:** can be used to enhance the stability and financial security of the customer.

**Tax Return:** look at all the schedules. Always obtain complete returns for self-employed customers and property owners. Look for depreciation and Car and Truck expenses to add back to the bottom line.

**CPA Letter:** accepted by many banks. For year-to-date income, for example.

**Bank Statements:** consistently high deposits for several months may verify income for a new business.

**Savings Accounts**: proof of secure 'liquid' assets is like money in the bank.

**Social Security Income:** can usually be verified with a copy of the 'award' letter, which describes the amount and the term of the benefits. the same is true for pensions and disability income.

---

They were so broke, they couldn't even pay attention.

- John R. du Teil
Investment Advisor

If you have a genuine source of income that is a little out of the ordinary, ask your buyer what she will accept as proof. A good buyer wants to help you make the deal.

If *you* believe the customer can pay for the car, don't give up.

# Notes

# The Credit Profile

Note the lower debt ratio for the less qualified customer.

A higher debt ratio is generally allowable for the customer with a substantial monthly income, since the disposable income is correspondingly greater.

Note the change from "**must** be favorable" to "**should** be favorable".

Lending institutions, just like people, realize that once you make an exception, rules are a matter of negotiation.

Here are typical underwriting criteria from a bank doing discount business with an automobile dealer:

| **Premium Contract Program**<br>"A" Paper | **Standard Contract Program**<br>"B" Paper |
|---|---|
| **EMPLOYMENT**<br>Minimum 2 years with current employer Exceptions may be made for a change within the same profession with no period of unemployment.<br><br>Self-employed applicants must have a minimum of 2 years in business. | **EMPLOYMENT**<br>Minimum 2 years with current employer Exceptions may be made for a change within the same profession with no period of unemployment.<br><br>Self-employed applicants must have a minimum of 2 years in business. |
| **INCOME**<br>Verified by a current paycheck stub for salaried employees.<br><br>Self-employed applicants must verify with a federal tax return. | **INCOME**<br>Verified by a current paycheck stub for salaried employees.<br><br>Self-employed applicants must verify with a federal tax return. |
| **DEBT TO INCOME RATIO**<br>Maximum not to exceed 44%<br><br>Must be calculated including the proposed instalment payment. | **DEBT TO INCOME RATIO**<br>Maximum not to exceed 40%<br><br>Must be calculated including the proposed instalment payment. |
| **RESIDENCY**<br>Minimum of 2 years at current address.<br><br>Exceptions may be made for newly purchased home, relocation due to job transfer or previous address was longer than 2 years. | **RESIDENCY**<br>Minimum of 2 years at current address.<br><br>Exceptions may be made for newly purchased home, relocation due to job transfer or previous address was longer than 2 years. |
| **CREDIT HISTORY**<br>Credit history as reported by TRW or CBI must be favorable. No exceptions.<br><br>Credit established for at least 5 years.<br><br>Established credit must include a bank.<br><br>No more than 6 active credit lines available, except when report shows that monthly balances are paid off monthly or are at a minimum.<br><br>No more than 5 inquiries in the last year. | **CREDIT HISTORY**<br>Credit history by TRW or CBI must be favorable, with minor exceptions.<br><br>Credit established for at least 5 years.<br><br>Established credit must include a bank.<br><br>Exceptions possible for 1 or 2 30-day delinquencies and 1 60-day late. Perhaps a collection account with no more than a $100 balance.<br><br>No more than 5 inquiries in the last year. |

> People are always blaming their circumstances for what they are. I don't believe in circumstances. The people who get on on this world are the people who get up and look for the circumstances they want, and, if they can't find them, make them.
>
> - George Bernard Shaw

**A finance manager should be an expert in credit.**
The real difference between "A" and "B" paper is obviously in the credit history. In fact, usually the difference between "A" paper and anything else is the credit history. The way to become an expert is not to take anything for granted. Look for positive information and substantiate it. You don't have to learn to look for *negative* information ... you won't be able to avoid it. When it looks negative, find out why.

**What a bank calls "criteria" are really guidelines written by an institutional credit manager who expects negotiation.**
You are expected to work on behalf of your customer. When you do that job well, you gain the respect of everyone involved in the process. The best finance managers are like alchemists ... they can turn lead into gold.

**Always run two different profiles.**
In California, the two most common are TRW and CBI. Often the information varies in each. There have been cases where a bankruptcy is reported on one bureau and the other showed no delinquency at all. Usually the reports will compliment each other. One will be more recent or show more detail. When building a case for a deal, you are in the information business. When one profile is stronger than the other, you should certainly make sure that the credit buyer is aware of that. It may not be standard procedure for the bank to run the particular report that you need them to see.

**Keep available the directories for each of the credit bureaus.**
You might need to look up a particular account in order to call and verify that a balance has been paid off or reduced. The customer may claim to know nothing about a stated delinquency, in which case you can call and perhaps clear it up. Know your contact at the bureau in case you need to call to clarify certain codes. Write your own subscriber number inthe book, since you will need to identify yourself when in contact with the agency.

Don't hesitate to follow this procedure when you are faced with a collection account that the customer doesn't acknowledge, a lien that needs to be released or a recently-paid past due balance. One telephone call can make the deal or change a "B" deal to an "A". You are the professional. With potentially marginal deals, always plan to have a conversation with the customer.

## The Customer Interview

This conversation should take place in the salesperson's office ... that way you can get up and leave at the end of the conversation. If the interview takes place in your office, and you decide not to deliver the car at that time, it may leave the customer feeling at a loss. When you go to the customer, it looks more like regular procedure. Do not close on rates and terms if you do not plan on delivering the car. You don't want to make promises you may not be able to keep, nor do you want the customer to take your hard work down the street to another dealer.

Resolve the deal on the spot if you can. Call the lender and get feedback on the deal you have put together. You probably won't get a commitment until the bank makes it own investigation, but you might get a storng enough 'feel' for how they will look at it to make your own decision about delivering the car.

The 'spot' delivery is another example of the value of a good finance manager. You know the lenders, you know the deal and often you enable the store to deliver a vehicle while the customer is still excited about her new car. Part of the learning process we all go through is to lose a deal to the more aggressive dealership who would deliver a questionable deal 'right now'. Your judgement in these situations is developed as part of your skills as a professional.

Have the discussion with the customer before you talk to the bank. The earlier in the process that you can give your credit buyer positve perceptions of your customer, the better off you are. It is always more difficult to change a mind than to make one up in the first place.

Begin the conversation with the conversation with the customer by pointing out all the positive apects of the deal: job stability, downpayment, previous car loans ... whatever it may be. Then focus on the problem: "There's just one or two things we need to clear up Mrs. Jones, so that I can explain your situation to the bank".

You want the customer to understand that you are the professional when it comes to successful underwriting, not because you fabricate a good story, but because you know what you're doing and you are very thorough. You believe that the customer had a problem with circumstances that were probably beyond her control and now that problem has been resolved. You believe in the customer and you are on his or her side.

---

If you aspire to be a good conversationalist, be an attentive listener.

To be interesting, be interested.

Ask the questions that the other person will enjoy answering.

Encourage them to talk about themselves and their accomplishments.

- Dale Carnegie

# The Credit Profile

Your focus during your conversation with the customer should not only be on what caused the problem, but what did the customer do to rectify the situation?

Has he talked to the lender invvolved?

Did she ultimately pay the charge-off?

Is there any correspondence, copies of which would speak well for the customer?

Would it be helpful to speak with the accountant?

With the business banker?

Is there a possible co-signer?

## Do your research before meeting the customer

- Look for recent inquiries. Has the customer been to other dealerships? Other banks?
- How far back does the credit history go? Do you have 4 or 5 years?
- What is the previous high credit, not counting real estate or equity loans?
- What is the debt ratio?
- Are there any car loans? How many?
- Are there problems centered around one particular time period?
- How is the credit before and after that time?

## Possible questions for the customer

- Do you have any credit other than what is reported here?
- Have you had any auto loans? Perhaps a credit union?
- Do you have any other sources of income?
- What does your last year's tax return show onthe bottom of the first page as Adjusted Gross Income?
- Is there a particular reason for the delinquencies?
- Do you have a business banker as a reference?
- Do you have a college degree? Do you have a student loan?
- Do you have reciepts or cancelled checks to show recent balances paid?
- Are stated balances currently accurate?
- Do you have stocks, certificates of deposit or savings accounts?
- Does your spouse work? Can we include that income or credit?
- Can you prove that a loan is actually being paid by the co-signer or by a business?
- Can a mortgage be offset by a rental agreement?
- More money down? A less expensive car? How much cash is available?

> Man is not the creature of circumstances.
>
> Circumstances are the creatures of men.
>
> - Benjamin Disraeli

Typical responses to your questions might be something like the following. It is important with credit negatives to put the problem accounts in context. If the credit was good before the trouble, and after the trouble, then the delinquencies can fairly be expected not to occur again.

**30 days late on one account:**
The customer was sending in the payment on the wrong date. He thought he had a grace period, like a house payment. Or perhaps there is a balance that is in dispute and consequently carried forward every month without his knowledge.

**30 days late on several accounts in one period:**
Probably the most common reason for this is a divorce. One spouse may have run the credit cards up to the maximum and then torn them up. Or funds may have been temporarily unavailable or probably tied up in attorney's fees. There may have been a death in the family, time spent out of the country or a suddenly dramatic financial loss.

**Charge-offs:**
Many of the same reasons apply ... the situation just got worse. The factor to look for here, besides the reason for the problem, is whether or not the customer finally met the obligation and paid the debt. If he did, it's a strong point in his favor.

**Voluntary Repossessions:**
Often this is a result of a dispute with a dealer. Perhaps the customer became unhappy with the deal and returned the car ... not understanding the repercussions to her credit.

**Involuntary Repossessions:**
Perhaps there was a misunderstanding and the vehicle was returned to the customer immediately. Every customer who has a repossession on his or her record will have a story to go with it.

**Bankruptcy:**
The worse the credit, the better the equity position has to be. See if you have a potential skip hazard. If you have 50% down and the customer has lived in the community, close to her nearest relatives and her personal references, you may be in good shape. Everyone understands a business reversal.

> Circumstances?
>
> I make circumstances!
>
> - Napoleon Bonaparte

If you have 50% down, but she just moved to your town from out of state and has no local references, you might have a problem. If the bankruptcy is the result of a failed business, the customer may have returned to a salaried position at which he or she is doing well. There may have been bad legal advice. Again, divorce may have been a factor. Whatever the reason, isolate the incident, surround it with positive factors and be persistent if you believe in the deal.

Be creative. Perhaps a letter from the customer directly to the bank might help establish credibility. Maybe an attorney could shed light could assist with an explanation. Customers in this position will be more flexible and cooperative than usual. Perhaps, on a less expensive car, the 50% downpayment would have more impact on the deal.

**Liens:**
Look for the line that shows the same lien released. Otherwise the customer may have to produce a "Statement of Lien Satisfied". These are available at city hall.

If it just happens that you cannot get a deal bought, let it be the bank's decision, not yours. Exhaust all sources, try everything you can think of. If you can't do it, no one else can. If it ever happens that you do lose a deal, and someone else makes it, find out what happened ... and don't make the same mistake again.

Remember the four C's to build a cae:

| | |
|---|---|
| CAPACITY | - Ability to pay |
| CREDIT ABILITY | - History of payment |
| CHARACTER | - Stability of the Borrower |
| COLLATERAL | - Equity for the Lender |

If you have less of one element, have more of the others. Don't just talk, Document your argument. Give your credit buyer evidence to support the decision to buy the deal.

## Other Credit Bureau Services

Talk with your credit services marketing representative. Find out what extra services are available. Some of the more common are:

**Online Directory**
Company names and contact information for creditors are listed.

**Mail Return Search**
A mailsearch system to seek better addresses in the database in case of returned mail or suspected fraud.

**Safescan**
A search for unusual patterns that may indicate application fraud.

**Social Security Number Search**
The system searches by social security number only, providing name, age, address and employment information.

**Trade Line Search**
The report groups accounts by type, which reduces the time it takes to calculate a debt ratio.

**Inquiry Activity Report**
Shows recent inquiries, identification information and employment verification. Useful for collections.

These are just a few examples of the services your credit bureau may provide. Contact you representative and find out what's new. Learn how to access the accounts listed on a bureau report directly. There is gold in them there hills.

# Notes

# Working with Lenders

*Nothing in the world can take the place of persistence.*

*Talent will not: nothing is more common than unsuccessful men with talent.*

*Genius will not: unrewarded genius is almost a proverb.*

*Education will not: the world is full of educated derelicts.*

*Persistence and determination alone are omnipotent.*

*- Calvin Coolidge*

**A good relationahip with a lender is worth more than any individual deal.**
Credit buyers are your lifeline. They can help you and they can hurt you. Most important to remember is that they are professionals, like yourself. They want to get through the day in the most agreeable way, like yourself. They want to make loans, build a solid portfolio and keep the risks to a minimum. Because they are professionals however, they do understand that there are risks. and they do understand, most of them, the pressures you are under. Just as in any relationship, you will get as good as you give. You want the buyers to take some of those risks with you.

**Get to know your sources, both institutions and individuals**.
Understand their priorities. Each one will be different. Know who will buy a deal if there's solid equity and be flexible on the debt ratio. Know who will over-advance if the customer is stronger than usual. Who will talk to the customer if necessary? Who will buy a qualified deal as-is.?

**Your credibility is a major asset when dealing with lenders**.
There are times, when a deal is borderline, that *your* perception of the customer will make a difference. If the credit buyer trusts you, and your judgement, he or she will take your opinion into account. After all, the lender does not meet the customer face to face. Establishing this kind of credibility takes time, and you will lose ground each time you pass on questionable information to the bank or play dumb about an element of the deal you obviously should have considered. Don't lie to your lenders.

**No one deal is a life or death situation.**
This is particularly true for the credit buyer, who is on the other end of the grind several times a day. Save your emotion for those deals when you legimately feel that you have a case that is not being heard.

**If you have the actual terms of the deal, include them in the submission.**
If you have proof of income, include that as well. Check your application for completeness. Call and make sure it was received.

**Develop a relationship with your credit buyer.**
Go to lunch with him or her. Talk about things other than business. *Listen* to the person. At times, when neither of you are too busy, update each other over the phone. You are both working toward the same goal. Once you have a relationship, keep it above the daily grind.

> I should never have made my success in life if I had not bestowed upon the least thing I have undertaken the same attention and care that I have bestowed upon the greatest.
>
> - Charles Dickens

**When it's a deal you believe in, take it to the top if you have to.**
When you have a deal that you truly believe has merit and you feel that the line officer is not treating it appropriately, ask her if she would mind if you took the deal to their supervisor. Don't just go over their head. Let the buyer know that you follow up on deals you believe in. do this graciously and do it every time. Don't do it for those deals that don't have the intrinsic merit. The buyer should understand that this is nothing personal, you are just doing your job. Sometimes it's a call they can't make on thier own and they will help you.

**When a source goes to extra lengths to help you, show your appreciation right away.**
When a buyer gives you that "as-is" approval you need, or steps up to an over-advance that makes your deal possible, respond by giving them a strong deal as soon as possible. When a bank accepts your explanation of a credit problem and buys the deal, make sure that the income verification they asked for is complete. give them the next deal. When you are helped, help back. When someone makes life easier for you, reciprocate as soon as you can.

**Work with several different sources.**
In these days of special lease programs, rebates and sub-vented factory rates, it seems that an unseen hand keeps pushing your deals to the captive sources. They take all the best paper and you make little, if any, reserve. Keep your sources competitive by sending the same deal to different banks. Don't send an application to a source you are not seriously considering. Be honest when one asks how the other treated a particular deal. Let a source know when they are not competitive in terms of rate, response time or stipulations. you are the customer here. Lending sources should be competing for your business.

**Develop a relationship with those who work in the funding department.**
Get to know the people who process your paperwork at the bank, as well those who verify insurance, check the documentation and fund the contracts. Check with them frequently and offer to help. Ask them to keep you up to date on anything that needs to be done to fund a deal. As always, if you help them, they will help you when they have the chance.

He who answers a matter before he hears it is not wise.

- Solomon

**Always negotiate your approvals.**
Submit a deal for a long term, and be prepared to accept a shorter term. Show less downpayment than you think you might be able to get if you pushed it. Offer to accept a higher buy rate, if you have room in the deal. Include a marginal deal with two good deals in a package. Sometimes you may not want to put all your cards on the table at once, especially if you know you are dealing with a source who is going to put conditions on your deal. If you need 'as-is' approval, perhaps more downpayment will help. Participate in the approval process. Don't just take instruction from the lender.

**Don't take 'No' for an answer.**
(Unless you knew the deal to be indefensible when you submitted it ... which is fair enough). Otherwise, you want to know what it will take to make a deal. Give a salesperson something to work with. A deal might take several days ... "I got this part of what you asked for, but I couldn't get that ...". The buyer may then compromise further ... "Can you at least get .....?" A good buyer will try to help when he or she sees the effort you are putting into a deal and may settle for a lesser amount financed, etc....Eventually there is a deal where there was not one before.

**If you have a good relationship with a buyer, ask for a favor.**
Only when you really need it. Perhaps you already deleivered the car or you found out that the tax return won't show all the income necessary because some of it was "under the table". Maybe you believe the customer's story about the life-changing divorce and you know the credit problem won't be repeated. the key again is simple. If you get a favor, return it right away.

**Periodically re-evaluate your Lender relationships.**
Sometimes where you send an application is clearly dictated by the terms of the deal - an 84 month ballon payment loan, for example, may only have one source. Those particular deals aside, you should take other factors into account. Who gives you the fastest callbacks? Who gives you the fewest stipulations? Who has the lowest buy rate? Who is the most understanding about isolated credit problems? Who went out of their way to help you recently? Occasionally there will be a situation where a bank has an unusually large capital situation (perhaps around IRA time) and wants to get that money out and working as soon as possible. Be careful not to become too reliant on one particular lending source. You may miss an opportunity elsewhere.

> Do what you can,
> with what you have,
> where you are.
>
> - Theodore Roosevelt

**Take notes, take notes, take notes.**

Who called? When? What exactly are the stipulations? If there aren't any, write that down. When you receive the actual documentation from the customer, if something is not as expected, discuss it with the buyer and get an ok. Don't just send in the deal and hope for the best. Take notes during the conversation with the customer about his credit. If it occurs to you that you should write something down, do it. Keep all notes in the deal.

**Deliver more than you promise.**

This is one of the cardinal rules followed by great salespeople. If you have *two* good deals with which to follow a marginal deal, send both. If you can get more down than the buyer required on a marginal deal, do it and put the buyer in a more secure position. Extra documentation, not required but supportive, is always welcomed. The value in this is that it demonstrates your good intentions.

# Notes

# Notes

# The Finance Contract

> Winning is not a sometime thing: it's an all time thing.
>
> You don't win once in a while, you don't do things right once in a while ...
> you do them right all the time. Winning is a habit.
>
> Unfortunately, so is losing.
>
> - Vince Lombardi

The business manager must understand financing ... not just financing the way your favorite bank would do it, but financing any way it can possibly be done. Just as lenders vary in the way they buy paper, they vary in the standards and policies surrounding contracts. One lender will over-advance, another will accept limited recourse endorsement, a third will buy 7-year balloon payments.... Writing loans is an area of technical expertise that should not be overlooked. No amount of sales ability can substitute for knowing your stuff technically. Being able to discern the customer's needs. knowing of a specific program which will meet those needs, and being able to structure the specific terms is a highly specialized, very valuable skill.

The customer is brought into your office expecting to meet an expert. By meeting those expectations, you immediately gain credibility. By extending the customer's options, you are providing a service he or she can not get anywhere else. At any given bank or credit union, the customer would only hear about what that particular lender had to offer.

**Computer Skills**
The ability to work with a computer is a special skill. The ability to work with people is a special skill. The ability to work with people and a computer simultaneously is what a finance manager gets paid for. To be able to change the terms back and forth on a worksheet screen, while keeping the customer's confidence that you are working *with* him or her, and not playing some sort of shell game, is a highly professional, very special skill. As long as the customer believes you are working on her behalf, you have the chance to answer all the questions at one time and make financial arrangements that work for everyone. On the machine, you need to be able to:

- Make a finance/lease comparison
- Roll a payment to the rate, the downpayment, the price, the service contract or the accessories
- Extend and shorten terms, changing the rate accordingly
- Add credit insurance automatically
- Show daily costs for additional insurance and service contract
- Show a cash conversion screen
- Show the finance charges for the various alternatives

When it is obvious that you know what you are doing, your customer is much more likely to have confidence in your advice.

> I have no use for bodyguards, but I have a very special use for two highly trained certified public accoutnants.
>
> - Elvis Presley

## Why finance through the Dealer?

Because you are there ... literally. Most customers will finance their car, one way or another. Your rates are competitive, your timing is convenient and you do in fact act as the customer's 'agent' in the transaction. You are an expert at shopping for loans and you can find terms comparable to any the customer can find on her own. All the paperwork is done at the same time. There is no need to take time out of a busy schedule to find a bank and endure another round of applications. By aligning himself with you, the customer is gaining an ally who will assist him in the future, should he need to re-schedule payments, refinance the car or conduct any business regarding the loan.

There is another reason that the customer may want to finance the purchase at a bank other than his own. If a customer finances a car at the bank where she has a checking account, the bank has a right to exercise what is known as a 'banker's lien'. If the account goes delinquent for any reason, the bank would have the right to take funds directly from the customer's checking account, without prior notice.

## Converting from a Credit Union loan

Some customers will be planning to finance their purchase through their local credit union. There are several reasons for them to consider an alternative:

- ❖ Some credit unions require non-cancellable payroll deductions
- ❖ A signature line of credit (perhaps only available at the credit union) is a handy safety net to keep open for emergencies
- ❖ The credit union may not report to a bureau ... therefore no credit enhancement ... usually a benefit of a car loan.
- ❖ Many credit unions use variable interest rates
- ❖ The credit union may not offer extended terms, or balloon payments, or over-advances or simple interest.
- ❖ Some credit unions only process applications once a week and the process is very time-consuming.
- ❖ Most credit unions do not offer leasing
- ❖ All the paperwork associated with the purchase can be done here and now.

Having a book on hand that shows current credit union rates and terms can often be valuable in conversion situations.

## Converting the Cash Customer

Most F&I computer programs now come with cash conversion software. After putting the deal in the machine as a finance deal, with suitable rate and downpayment, suggest to the customers that they consider investing most of the cash they were planning to spend on what is, after all, a depreciating item. Ask what would be considered a reasonable return on investment - conservative but realistic. A 9% return on $10,000 would be conservative. It is important that the rate of return, whatever it is, be the customers' idea, so that they will find your proposition credible. Enter the suggestion on the appropriate line in the program. A cash conversion print-out might look like this:

> In talking with people, don't begin by discussing the things on which you differ.
>
> Begin by emphasizing - and keep on emphasizing - the things on which you agree.
>
> Keep emphasizing, if possible, that you are both striving for the same end and that your only difference is one of method and not of purpose.
>
> Get the other person saying "Yes, yes" at the outset.
>
> - Dale Carnegie

**The customer can save over $10,000 by financing the car.**

---

August 31, 1991
Customer, John

| | | | | | |
|---|---|---|---|---|---|
| 1 Deal No | 1001 | 21 AOR | 6.39 | | |
| 2 Deal Dte | 08/31/91 | 22 APR | 11.50 | | |
| 3 Stock No | 7000 | 23 Tax Rate | 7.00 | | |

| | | | | | |
|---|---|---|---|---|---|
| Price | 44000 | Trade | 3500 | Amt Fin | 44087.45 |
| Access | | Payoff | 2000 | Fin Chg | 14087.95 |
| Doc Fee | 35 | Equity | 1500 | Tot Pmts | 58175.40 |
| Txbl Smog | | Pup #1 | | Df Pmt Price | 64675.40 |
| Tax | 3082.45 | Pup #2 | | Rate | 11.50 |
| Luxury Tax | 1400 | Pup #3 | | Term | 60 |
| Warr Prem | 1295 | Rebate | | Payment | 969.59 |
| FI Access Price | | Cash Down | 5000 | Balloon | |
| Cash Price | 49812.45 | Total Down | 6500 | Year | 91 |
| Lic Fees | 775 | | | | |
| Total | 50587.45 | Monthly Pmt | 969.59 | | |

Comparison for: John Customer

| The Cost of Paying Cash | | The Cost of Financing | |
|---|---|---|---|
| Investment | 44087.45 | Amount Financed | 44087.45 |
| Rate of Return | 9.00 | APR | 11.50 |
| Investment Period | 60 | Loan Term | 60 |
| **Interest Earned** | **24939.43** | **Finance Charge** | **14087.95** |

IT COSTS $10851.48 MORE TO PAY CASH THAN IT DOES TO FINANCE.

Financing is an inflation hedge, since you are paying back the loan in tomorrow's cheaper dollars.

**The return on the investment is greater than the cost of the money because the interest on the investment is compounded.**

The interest rate charged on the loan, although it is higher, is charged on a balance that is *declining* every day. The interest rate on the investment is paid on a balance that is *increasing* every day. To close this presentation, you might point out that the loan itself is simple interest, so that the customer retains the option to pay the loan off without penalty.

### Establishing a credit rating

A secondary benefit to financing the purchase of a car is the opportunity to establish credit. Perhaps the customer has only a couple of small credit accounts. By investing some cash and using the rest to make a sizeable downpayment, she can establish credit fairly quickly. To raise a credit limit in the traditional way, by applying to raise credit card limits once a year ... $500 or $1000 at a time ... can take several years. It is a well-known "Catch-22" in the credit world that you can't borrow a lot of money unless you have borrowed a lot of money. Who knows whether, three or four years down the road, the customer may have a need to borrow a larger sum of money for some reason? Perhaps he or she might want to start a business or expand their current enterprise. The future is unpredictable and even if the credit were never used, it is an additional option to have available for emergencies.

### CoSigners

Some lenders are still agreeable to using co-signers to strengthen a deal. Generally speaking, banks want co-signers to be close relatives. The more distant the relationship of the co-signer to the buyer, the less obligation the co-signer is likely to feel in the event of delinquency. *Cosigners compensate for lack of credit, not lack of income.* Lenders vary on their policy as to whether cosigners can compensate for *bad* credit. If the problem in the credit history is understandable, the lender may treat the customer as if she had no credit at all and then a cosigner will help. However, if a customer clearly can not afford the car, a cosigner will not help. Arranging cosigned loans is definitely a service in which the F&I manager should specialize. Most people only buy six or seven cars in a lifetime and everyone has to start somewhere.

An automobile purchase is an important event for the customer. It is not a decision he or she comes to easily, and the opportunity should be maximized. There are alternatives to spending all one's money on a depreciating asset. The 'safety net' is a simple interest contract, which can be paid off at any time without penalty

---

The most important part of the sales process is the salesperson .... With a deep personal belief in what you're selling, you will be able to communicate and transfer that feeling to the prospect.

- Zig Ziglar

## One Pay Contracts

The traditional way to deliver a car to a customer who absolutely insists on getting her own financing has been to write a 'One Pay' contract. This is a normal finance contract, with payment terms and an extra line added that allows the option of "One payment of $XX", where X = the amount financed.

*Smile*

*- Dale Carnegie*

'One Pay or" contracts are no longer reliable insurance for a 'spot' delivery.

Recently, a new civil law has gone into effect that makes this a potentially ineffective way to deliver cars. If a customer takes delivery of a vehicle with the understanding that he will obtain his own financing and then he is unable to obtain that financing, the customer has the right to rescind the contract. This right is extended for the life of the contract. If, after two years, the customer finds reason to be unhappy with the car, and recalls that the dealership financed the car after he did not get his own financing, the customer may still rescind the contract. Consequently, lenders are now reluctant to buy contracts containing the 'One Pay' clause. If you deliver the car on this basis, and the customer does not obtain his own financing, you may find yourself with an uncashable contract.

As an alternative, you might deliver the car on a regular contract, with a promise to wait five days, and have the customer sign an addendum. You might do a contract and a purchase order. Check with you Dealer and with the company attorney on policy. However you do it, don't deliver a car without a cashable contract.

> The worlds we manage to get inside our heads are mostly worlds of words.
>
> - Wendell Johnson

## Business Loans

A loan to a business always requires a guarantor. The exceptions would be those million-dollar companies with public financial statements. Lenders vary on policy regarding loans to businesses but it is good practice to routinely look for a guarantor. If the company is incorporated, the guarantor should be a corporate officer and must be authorized by corporate resolution to sign the specific contract on behalf of the company. Each lender has their own "Corporate Resolution to Borrow" form. Usually, this form is signed by the Corporate Secretary. If a person occupies all three corporate offices herself, most lenders will accept the form with just the one signature in both places. Financial statements and tax returns will be required.

The most common way to add a guarantor is to put that person's name on the cosigner line of the contract. The customer signs one side of the contract on behalf of the business (personal signature following business name) and the other side personally. The business must show sufficient stability and income to pay for the car, but often such loans are approved primarily on the strength of the guarantor. Guarantors must meet the usual credit approval criteria. In the case of a sole proprietorship, most lenders will allow the contract to be written with a DBA (Doing Business As) name without requiring additional documentation. or guarantee.

## Simple Interest

Simple interest loans are becoming increasingly common in this age of service-to-the-customer, since they generally provide for a lower payoff at early termination. The essential character of a simple interest loan is that the interest is charged against the outstanding balance. As soon as there is no more balance, there is no more interest. It is not a payoff calculated by a formula, such as the Rule of 78's. The Rule of 78's guarantees a certain yield to the bank by charging more for the loan at the beginning of the term. With a simple interest loan, there may be a penalty only if the loan is paid off before the first payment is due. Obviously more interest is charged at the beginning with simple interest too, since the outstanding balance is highest at the start of the loan. Those customers who are familiar with automobile loans will be aware of the difference and know that simple interest offers more options.

All loans over 60 months are required by law to be simple interest loans. When disclosing the loan to the customer, emphasize that payments should be made on time, even though there may be a 'grace period'.

## Amortization Schedule 1

It is handy to be able to produce an amortization table for a loan, if your computer service has the program available. It can help when you have to calculate a payoff. It can also be valuable information for a customer who just has to know everything about possible about a loan before he will do business.

The table shows how much of each payment goes to principal and how much to interest.

Note how the interest charges are greater at the beginning of the loan - because the interest rate is being charged against a higher balance.

### Simple Interest Contract @ 10%
(Payoff is Ending Balance)

Principal $10,000   Rate 10.00%   Months 48   Payment $253.63
Total Payments $12,174.04   Total Interest $2,174.04

| Month | Begin.Bal. | End.Bal. | Total Paid | Interest | Principal Payment |
|---|---|---|---|---|---|
| 1 | 10,000.00 | 9829.71 | 253.63 | 83.33 | 170.29 |
| 2 | 9829.71 | 9658.00 | 253.63 | 81.91 | 171.71 |
| 3 | 9658.00 | 9484.85 | 253.63 | 80.48 | 173.14 |
| 4 | 9484.85 | 9310.27 | 253.63 | 79.04 | 174.59 |
| 5 | 9310.27 | 9134.23 | 253.63 | 77.59 | 176.04 |
| 6 | 9134.23 | 8956.72 | 253.63 | 76.12 | 177.51 |
| 7 | 8956.72 | 8777.73 | 253.63 | 74.64 | 178.99 |
| 8 | 8777.73 | 8597.26 | 253.63 | 73.15 | 180.48 |
| 9 | 8597.26 | 8415.27 | 253.63 | 71.64 | 181.98 |
| 10 | 8415.27 | 8231.78 | 253.63 | 70.13 | 183.50 |
| 11 | 8231.78 | 8046.75 | 253.63 | 68.60 | 185.03 |
| **12** | **8046.75** | **7860.18** | **253.63** | **67.06** | **186.57** |
| 13 | 7860.18 | 7672.05 | 253.63 | 65.50 | 188.12 |
| 14 | 7672.05 | 7482.36 | 253.63 | 63.93 | 189.69 |
| 15 | 7482.36 | 7291.09 | 253.63 | 62.35 | 191.27 |
| 16 | 7291.09 | 7098.22 | 253.63 | 60.76 | 192.87 |
| 17 | 7098.22 | 6903.75 | 253.63 | 59.15 | 194.47 |
| 18 | 6903.75 | 6707.65 | 253.63 | 57.53 | 196.09 |
| 19 | 6707.65 | 6509.92 | 253.63 | 55.90 | 197.73 |
| 20 | 6509.92 | 6310.55 | 253.63 | 54.25 | 199.38 |
| 21 | 6310.55 | 6109.51 | 253.63 | 52.59 | 201.04 |
| 22 | 6109.51 | 5906.80 | 253.63 | 50.91 | 202.71 |
| 23 | 5906.80 | 5702.39 | 253.63 | 49.22 | 204.40 |
| **24** | **5702.39** | **5496.29** | **253.63** | **47.52** | **206.11** |
| 25 | 5496.29 | 5288.47 | 253.63 | 45.80 | 207.82 |
| 26 | 5288.47 | 5078.91 | 253.63 | 44.07 | 209.56 |
| 27 | 5078.91 | 4867.61 | 253.63 | 42.32 | 211.30 |
| 28 | 4867.61 | 4654.55 | 253.63 | 40.56 | 213.06 |
| 29 | 4654.55 | 4439.71 | 253.63 | 38.79 | 214.84 |
| 30 | 4439.71 | 4223.08 | 253.63 | 37.00 | 216.63 |
| 31 | 4223.08 | 4004.65 | 253.63 | 35.19 | 218.43 |
| 32 | 4004.65 | 3784.39 | 253.63 | 33.37 | 220.35 |
| 33 | 3784.39 | 3562.30 | 253.63 | 31.54 | 222.09 |
| 34 | 3562.30 | 3338.36 | 253.63 | 29.69 | 223.94 |
| 35 | 3338.36 | 3112.56 | 253.63 | 27.82 | 225.81 |
| **36** | **3112.56** | **2884.87** | **253.63** | **25.94** | **227.69** |
| 37 | 2884.87 | 2655.28 | 253.63 | 24.04 | 229.59 |
| 38 | 2655.28 | 2423.79 | 253.63 | 22.13 | 231.50 |
| 39 | 2423.79 | 2190.36 | 253.63 | 20.20 | 233.43 |
| 40 | 2190.36 | 1954.98 | 253.63 | 18.25 | 235.37 |
| 41 | 1954.98 | 1717.65 | 253.63 | 16.29 | 237.33 |
| 42 | 1717.65 | 1478.34 | 253.63 | 14.31 | 239.31 |
| 43 | 1478.34 | 1237.03 | 253.63 | 12.32 | 241.31 |
| 44 | 1237.03 | 993.72 | 253.63 | 10.31 | 243.32 |
| 45 | 993.72 | 748.37 | 253.63 | 8.28 | 245.34 |
| 46 | 748.37 | 500.98 | 253.63 | 6.24 | 247.37 |
| 47 | 500.98 | 251.53 | 253.63 | 4.17 | 249.45 |
| 48 | 251.53 | 0.00 | 253.63 | 2.10 | 251.63 |

## Rule of 78's

This kind of loan is also called "sum of the digits" financing. The calculations treat the loan as if it were divided into 78 parts, and then paid over the term of the loan. As with simple interest, the greater part of the finance charges is paid at the beginning of the loan. For example, an installment loan for 12 months would add up exactly: 12+11+10+9+8+7+6+5+4+3+2+1=78.

In the first month, before making any payments, the customer has the use of the whole amount borrowed and therefore pays 12/78's of the total interest in the first payment. In the second month, she has the use of 11 parts of the loan and so pays 11/78's of the interest ... and so on to the final installment, which is 1/78 interest.

There is a formula that can be used to calulate a payoff. Whenever a loan is paid of early, of course the principal is repaid in full. It is the interest charges for the unused period of time that may be refunded. The formula first calculates how much of each payment represents interest and then multiplies that by the number of unused payments. Where X equals the number of payments remaining on the loan, the formula is

$X/2 \times (X+1)$ = the fraction of each payment that is interest.

For a $10,000 loan over 48 months @ 10%

$48/2 \times (48+1) = 24 \times 49 = 1176$

The first payment will then represent 48/1176 or 4.1% of the interest, the second payment will be 47/1176 or 4% and so on....

If the customer wants to pay off the loan after a year, and there's no access to an amortization schedule, the amount of interest to be refunded can be calculated if the number of months remaining is known. For example, on the above loan, after 12 months, 36 months are remaining so:

$36/2 \times (36+1) = 18 \times 37 = 666$ parts of interest remaining,

666/1176 or 56.6% of the interest will be refund.
56.6% x $2174.04 (Total Interest) = $1230.51

Simple Interest: first 12 months cost $903.69
Rule of 78's first 12 months cost $943.53

---

*The payoff estimate should always come from the customer.*

*Only under special circumstances should the dealership assume responsibility for the figure used as a payoff estimate ... when the actual figure cannot be obtained from the lienholder.*

*If you quote a figure that turns out to be incorrect, you may find it difficult to collect the difference. The customer will remind you that it was your figure in the first place.*

*Even though you may have a computer program to do the calculations for you, there may be late charges, insurance add-ons or other fees and penalties which you did not take into account.*

*In both cases, simple interest and Rule of 78's, although the loan is paid off 25% of the way through the term, more than 25% of the interest is paid.*

*The simple interest loan may be seen as not having the built-in 'penalty' inherent in the Rule of 78's, although the difference is not great.*

## Amortization Schedule 2

Making extra payments on an auto loan, or paying a large sum at one time during the course of the loan, does not reduce the monthly payment. Only when the loan is completely paid off is the interest charge reduced.

Early or increased payments will reduce the term of the loan, which will ultimately reduce the interest. So the customer may not see the benefit of extra payments until near the end of the loan term.

Advise the customer to keep any extra money until the loan can be paid off completely.

There would also be a refund of any unused insurance premium at that time.

**Simple Interest Contract @ 11.75%**
Principal $10,000   Rate 11.75%   Months 60
Payment $221.18   Total Payments $13270.80
Total Interest $3270.80

| Payment | Principal | Interest |
|---|---|---|
| 1. 221.18 | 123.26 | 97.92 |
| 2. 221.18 | 124.47 | 96.71 |
| 3. 221.18 | 125.69 | 95.49 |
| 4. 221.18 | 126.92 | 94.26 |
| 5. 221.18 | 128.16 | 93.02 |
| 6. 221.18 | 129.42 | 91.76 |
| 7. 221.18 | 130.69 | 90.50 |
| 8. 221.18 | 131.96 | 89.22 |
| 9. 221.18 | 133.26 | 87.92 |
| 10. 221.18 | 134.56 | 86.62 |
| 11. 221.18 | 135.88 | 85.30 |
| 12. 221.18 | 137.21 | 83.97 |
| 13. 221.18 | 138.55 | 82.63 |
| 14. 221.18 | 139.91 | 81.27 |
| 15. 221.18 | 141.28 | 79.90 |
| 16. 221.18 | 142.66 | 78.52 |
| 17. 221.18 | 144.06 | 77.12 |
| 18. 221.18 | 145.47 | 75.71 |
| 19. 221.18 | 146.90 | 74.29 |
| 20. 221.18 | 148.33 | 72.85 |
| 21. 221.18 | 149.79 | 71.40 |
| 22. 221.18 | 151.25 | 69.93 |
| 23. 221.18 | 152.73 | 68.45 |
| 24. 221.18 | 154.23 | 66.95 |
| 25. 221.18 | 155.74 | 65.44 |
| 26. 221.18 | 157.26 | 63.92 |
| 27. 221.18 | 158.80 | 62.38 |
| 28. 221.18 | 160.36 | 60.82 |
| 29. 221.18 | 161.93 | 59.25 |
| 30. 221.18 | 163.51 | 57.67 |
| 31. 221.18 | 165.12 | 56.07 |
| 32. 221.18 | 166.73 | 54.45 |
| 33. 221.18 | 168.37 | 52.82 |
| 34. 221.18 | 170.01 | 51.17 |
| 35. 221.18 | 171.68 | 49.50 |
| 36. 221.18 | 173.36 | 47.82 |
| 37. 221.18 | 175.06 | 46.12 |
| 38. 221.18 | 176.77 | 44.41 |
| 39. 221.18 | 178.50 | 42.68 |
| 40. 221.18 | 180.25 | 40.93 |
| 41. 221.18 | 182.01 | 39.17 |
| 42. 221.18 | 183.80 | 37.38 |
| 43. 221.18 | 185.60 | 35.58 |
| 44. 221.18 | 187.41 | 33.77 |
| 45. 221.18 | 189.25 | 31.93 |
| 46. 221.18 | 191.10 | 30.08 |
| 47. 221.18 | 192.97 | 28.21 |
| 48. 221.18 | 194.86 | 26.32 |
| 49. 221.18 | 196.77 | 24.41 |
| 50. 221.18 | 198.70 | 22.48 |
| 51. 221.18 | 200.64 | 20.54 |
| 52. 221.18 | 202.61 | 18.57 |
| 53. 221.18 | 204.59 | 16.59 |
| 54. 221.18 | 206.59 | 14.59 |
| 55. 221.18 | 208.62 | 12.56 |
| 56. 221.18 | 210.66 | 10.52 |
| 57. 221.18 | 212.72 | 8.46 |
| 58. 221.18 | 214.81 | 6.38 |
| 59. 221.18 | 216.91 | 4.27 |
| 60. 221.18 | 219.30 | 2.15 |
| 13,271.06 | 10,000 | 3,271.07 |

**$10,000 Invested @ 9% Compounded Monthly**

| | |
|---|---|
| 1. | 75.00 |
| 2. | 150.53 |
| 3. | 226.69 |
| 4. | 303.09 |
| 5. | 381.18 |
| 6. | 459.04 |
| 7. | 537.48 |
| 8. | 616.52 |
| 9. | 696.14 |
| 10. | 776.36 |
| 11. | 857.18 |
| 12. | 938.61 |
| 13. | 1020.65 |
| 14. | 1103.31 |
| 15. | 1186.58 |
| 16. | 1201.48 |
| 17. | 1355.01 |
| 18. | 1440.17 |
| 19. | 1525.97 |
| 20. | 1612.42 |
| 21. | 1699.51 |
| 22. | 1787.26 |
| 23. | 1875.66 |
| 24. | 1964.73 |
| 25. | 2054.46 |
| 26. | 2144.87 |
| 27. | 2235.96 |
| 28. | 2327.73 |
| 29. | 2420.19 |
| 30. | 2513.96 |
| 31. | 2607.81 |
| 32. | 2702.37 |
| 33. | 2797.64 |
| 34. | 2893.62 |
| 35. | 2990.33 |
| 36. | 3087.75 |
| 37. | 3185.91 |
| 38. | 3284.81 |
| 39. | 3384.44 |
| 40. | 3484.82 |
| 41. | 3585.96 |
| 42. | 3687.86 |
| 43. | 3790.51 |
| 44. | 3893.94 |
| 45. | 3988.15 |
| 46. | 4103.13 |
| 47. | 4208.91 |
| 48. | 4315.47 |
| 49. | 4331.01 |
| 50. | 4422.84 |
| 51. | 4639.99 |
| 52. | 4749.79 |
| 53. | 4860.42 |
| 54. | 4971.87 |
| 55. | 5084.16 |
| 56. | 5197.29 |
| 57. | 5311.27 |
| 58. | 5426.11 |
| 59. | 5441.80 |
| 60. | 5658.36 |
| 5658.36 Interest Earned | |

*Let us never negotiate out of fear.*

*But let us never fear to negotiate.*

*- John F. Kennedy*

**Assigning the contract.**
Most dealers will limit their assignment of contracts to non-recourse, meaning that once the contract is purchased by the lending institution, that institution has no recourse to the dealer if the customer fails to pay. There are other options open to the dealer, but choosing them is strictly a matter of policy, to be set by the owner. There may occasionally be a benefit to limited recourse. by sharing a certain amount of liability, the dealership may be able to finance an otherwise un-financeable deal or buy the money at a discounted rate. When assuming any liability on a deal, look for the worst case. Is the buyer a skip hazard? What if the car comes back? You must hear it from the dealer if he or she wants to play that game at all. The key is usually a large downpayment. Lenders vary in their recourse policies, just as they do in everything else.

**Non-Recourse:** there is no recourse to the dealer, regardless of the customer's payment record. The only recourse may be the charge-back of prepaid finance reserve and/or refund of insurance premiums. Any other liability belongs to the lender. Many national banks are strictly non-recourse.

**90 Day Repurchase:** the dealer endorses the contract to the extent that she will repurchase the collateral (vehicle) for the remaining contract balance, in the event of default by the customer. The lender typically has 90 days from the initial date of delinquency to repossess and return the vehicle to the dealer.

**Limited Repurchase:** with some lenders, the extent of recourse to the dealer is negotiable. The dealer may recourse or guarantee a contract for only part of the term, or part of the balance. Perhaps 20% recourse. Or guarantee of the residual or the over-advance. Many things are possible and these are oftern overlooked.

**Guarantee:** the dealer promises to pay the contract balance to the lender upon demand, regardless of condition or status of the collateral. This happens about as often as the giving away of a free car for everyone named Dave.

Most of your loans will be non-recourse. However, by being skillful and creative, sometimes you can deliver a deal that seemed impossible. This, perhaps more than anything else, is the sign of a first-class Business Manager.

## Documentation

A major reason for funding delays is the absence of one or more documents stipulated by the bank upon approval. The finance manager must ensure that each package to a lender contains:

- Original, complete customer statement with signatures
- Contract, complete with initials and signatures
- Copy of factory invoice or MSRP sticker
- Copy of Repair Order or Due Bill documenting value-added options
- Insurance information, sufficient for verification
- Income verification, if required
- Financial statement, if company
- Corporate Resolution to Borrow, if a corporation
- Copy of extended service contract, for leases
- Copy of Report of Sale, showing lender as lienholder (for leases)
- Sales tax (on cap reduction) or Luxury tax (for leases)
- Copy of worksheet (for leases)
- Authorized dealer signature

At least 30% of funding delays are the result of inadequate attention to insurance verification. Problems can be:

- No contact person or phone number available to the lender
- Improper amount of coverage
- Lender receives incorrect contact information
- Customer has not personally notified the agent

Lack of verification of appropriate coverage is costing some dealers thousands of dollars. Use the insurance notification card. Verify the insurance yourself before you send out the package. Don't ignore the problem.

# Notes

# The Lease

> The old idea of a good bargain was a transaction in which one man got the better of another.
>
> The new idea of a good contract is a transaction which is good for both parties to it.
>
> - Louis D. Brandeis
> U.S. Supreme Court Justice

Leasing sources vary more in their requirements than your sources for retail financing. Since they are taking more of a risk with their money, lessors are generally more stringent in their credit standards. The real differences are in the specifics of the various programs. They may differ in several aspects: residual percentages, mark-ups, security deposits, accessory allowance, cap reductions and cosigner policies. That is why there is no generic lease form that is acceptable to all banks ... as there is with a retail contract.

**It is essential to stay up to date. you need to know which source is best for a particular vehicle and customer, before you work out the terms.** A 5% difference in residual might make or break a deal. Perhaps the customer does not want to provide a cap reduction in order to lower the payment, but will provide several *refundable* security deposits that would lower the rate. The key to successful leasing is to know your sources.

**Do not discuss a lease with a customer until you have done a credit evaluation.** It is much more difficult to get a customer to step up to a higher payment, when you discover he doesn't qualify for a lease, than it is to offer the option of a lower payment after presenting retail terms. Obviously a lower payment on a lease looks much more attractive to a customer who has seen a higher payment first.

**Take the process step by step.** Be sure the customer is qualified. Discuss the idea of leasing and be sure that the customer appreciates the concept before you introduce specific terms. As with any presentation, you should close the door to each higher level objection as you lay the groundwork. When you finally present a payment, you don't want the customer to retreat to an objection against leasing itself.

**Leasing is most appropriate for those customers who don't plan on keeping the car more than four or five years**. They appreciate the benefit of investing their money, rather than putting a large cash payment down on a depreciating asset. They like the fact that, with the lower lease payment, they can 'drive more car for the money'. They are sophisticated enough not to be intimidated by the residual at the end of the term. And they understand the value of a closed-end lease.

Counsel your customer about leasing. Buyers who are not familiar with the benefits will appreciate your advice.

## Questions about Leasing

A finance manager probably gets asked more questions about leasing than anything else. It is important to understand leasing technically.

### How do banks determine the residuals?
Banks base estimates on the future wholesale value of their leased vehicles primarily based on their experience at used car auctions around the country.

### Can I get out of a lease early?
Yes. However, am amortization schedule would show that most of your payment at the beginning goes toward the lease fee. If you began the lease with the minimum fees (no cap reduction), then you should not expect to have equity in the vehicle until at least halfway through the term of the lease.

### Can I buy the car at the end of the lease?
Yes. For either market value or residual value, depending on the type of lease. You would pay the sales tax on the balance at that time.

### Can I refinance the car at the end of the leae?
Yes. As long as you have a good payment record on the lease, most banks will offer that option automatically.

### Is the lease assumable?
Usually yes. It depends on the individual bank. The finance manager will be able to assist in that process, should the customer wish to transfer the lease.

### Can I change the residual?
Yes. You can lower it (about 25% at most), however, there may be nothing to be gained if ownership is desired. Some banks will allow purchase at residual value or a percentage of Kelly Blue Book, whichever is greater.

### Does the lease cover maintenance?
No. Not unless a specific written agreement is included.

### What is the interest rate?
There isn't one. A lease is not a purchase. The fees are calculated using a lease factor. In some states, California for example, lenders are specifically instructed to make the difference bewteen a lease and a purchase very clear. A lease factor is a charge for the use of the vehicle. Factors vary from bank to bank.

---

*If a man is brusque in his manner, others will not cooperate.*

*If he is agitated in his words, they will awaken no echo in others.*

*If he asks for something without having first established a proper relationship, it will not be given to him.*

- I Ching

**If there is a change in the tax rate in my county, will the tax on my payment change?**

Yes. Since you are paying for the use of the vehicle from month to month, sales tax is not locked in at the beginning of the lease.

**Can I walk away at the end of the lease?**
Yes ... on a closed-end lease, assuming normal miles and reasonable wear and tear. On an open-end lease, you have to make up the difference in value, if the vehicle is worth less than the residual at the end of the term.

**What's the difference between a closed-end lease and an open-end lease?**
On a closed-end lease, the lessee may buy the vehicle at the end of the lease for the residual value, assuming normal miles and reasonable wear and tear. Or the customer may return the vehicle to the bank with no further obligation.

On an open-end lease. the customer is responsible for the residual value instead of the bank. If the car does not re-sell for the residual value, the cusotmer makes up the difference. There is no option to simply return the car and walk away. If the car sells for more than the residual, the lessee is entitled to that difference and may still buy the car at term.

**What are the mileage restrictions on a lease?**
Typically mileage is restricted to under 18,000 miles a year. Miles driven in excess of the bank's limit are subject to a charge of anywhere from 12 to 25 cents a mile. If the customer anticipates driving more than the minimum, a mileage allowance is subtracted from the residual value. For example, 5,000 extra miles a year on a five-year lease = 25,000 extra miles. At 12 cents a mile, the extra mileage charge is $3000. This amount is subtracted from the residual value ... and the payment rises accordingly. This kind of formula is designed to cover the extra depreciation by the end of the lease.

**Is my lease deductible as a business expense?**
It may be easier to list a lease as a monthly business expense. It is best to consult with your CPA.

**Can I lease with no downpayment at all?**
Yes. Your payment will include your initial fees.

**What is "reasonable wear and tear"?**
The specifics are spelled out in each bank's lease form. Usually the explanation includes inoperative parts, mismatched paint, dents, scratches over two inches long, windshield cracks and so on.... No bank expects the car to be perfect.

## Insurance Requirements

Since the leasing source is legally the registered owner of the vehicle, they require more than the minimum insurance. Typically, stipulated coverage is:

$100,000 Collision
$300,000 Liability
$50,000   Property Damage
$1000 deductible maximum

The source will be "additionally insured" and "loss payee".

*30% of funding delays are the result of insurance complications.*

## Residual Calculation

Check each source carefully for their residual calculation formula. Some banks will allow you to include accessories at retail price, some will only allow a set amount. Some sources will allow you to include dealer preparation and bank mark-up charges in the calculation, some will not. Banks also vary in the amount of confidence they have in the resale value of certain vehicles. Know which banks give the highest residuals for your line of cars.

## Luxury Tax

At the present time (October 1991), banks are treating the luxury tax in a variety of different ways. It may be required up front with the lease fees or included in the cap cost. If it is inthe cap cost, you should adjust the sales tax, so that the customer is not paying sales tax on the luxury tax - although not all banks require this adjustment yet. If you have to make the adjustment so that the lease program in your machine will print out the proper tax on the form, it can be done this way:

*If you collect luxury tax up front, send a check for that amount to the bank with the lease package.*

*If the bank insists that the luxury tax be capitalized, collect exactly the same amount as a cap reduction.*

*Of course, luxury tax is not included in the residual calculation.*

If the sales tax before adding the luxury tax is $35 monthly
and the sales tax after adding the luxury tax is $38.50 monthly

Then the adjustment factor is 35/38.50 = .9090
If the old tax rate is 8.25%
then the tax rate x the adjustment factor = 8.25 x .9090 = 7.499%

Entering this new rate in the program will correct the tax calculation. You may then need to manually change the printed tax rate from 7.499 to 8.25. the new payment will be higher as a result of the addition of the luxury tax, but the additional sales tax will have been removed.

> There went out a decree from Caesar Augustus that all the world should be taxed.
>
> - New Testament

## Gap Insurance

In today's leasing market, with no downpayments and 60 month terms, the insurance payoff in the event of a total loss may not completely cover the lessee's financial obligation. If, in the event of an accident, the vehicle is considered a total loss, comprehensive and collision insurance will pay the actual cash value of the car. There may be a significant difference between the actual cash value of the car and the payoff balance on the lease, especially in the first half of the term.

Many lease source now provide 'gap'insurance, in the event of total loss due to collision or theft, the lessee is absolved of all responsibility for any deficiency, in case the standard insurance fails to satisfy the outstanding balance. The only cost to the lessee would be the cost of the deductible on the insurance policy. This is a point in favor of leasing, with those banks that include loss protection as part of the lease package.

## Lease payment calculation

A lease payment is made up of three parts: the average monthly lease charge, the average monthly depreciation and the sales tax. The amount of payment that is lease fee and the amount that is depreciation will vary every month. An amortization schedule would show more of the payment going toward the lease fee inthe beginning of the term and more going toward the principal in the second half. The calculation is as follows:

> Remember to include the bank fee in the initial value

| AVERAGE MONTHLY LEASE CHARGE | |
|---|---|
| Initial Value of Vehicle | $21,268 |
| Less Cap Reduction | - 1,500 |
| Plus Service Contract | + 800 |
| Balance Subject to Lease Charge | $20,568 |
| Plus Residual Value @ 44% | + 7,558 |
| TOTAL | $28,126 |
| Multiplied by Lease Factor | x .00440 |
| Average Monthly Lease Charge | $123.75 |

| AVERAGE MONTHLY DEPRECIATION | |
|---|---|
| Balance Subject to Lease Charge | $20,568 |
| Less Residual Value | - 7,558 |
| Total Lease Depreciation | $13,010 |
| Divided by Lease term | ÷ 48 |
| Average Monthly Depreciation | $271.04 |

**Formula:**
Balance subject to lease charge
+ residual value
x lease factor
= average monthly lease charge

Balance subject to lease charge
- residual value
÷ by term
= average monthly depreciation

average monthly lease charge
+ average monthly depreciation
= base monthly payment (Plus Tax)

| TOTAL MONTHLY PAYMENT | |
|---|---|
| Average Monthly Lease Charge | $123.75 |
| Average Monthly Depreciation | +271.04 |
| Base Monthly Payment | $394.79 |
| Plus Tax @ 8.25% | + 32.57 |
| Total Monthly Payment | $427.36 |

# The Lease

## Leasing vs. Financing

> If you aren't fired with enthusiasm, you'll be fired with enthusiasm.
>
> - Vince Lombardi

### Finance: $5000 Down

| | | | |
|---|---|---|---|
| Price | 24135.90 | Down | 5000.00 |
| Doc | 35.00 | Rate | 11.50 |
| Tax | 1994.10 | Fin Chg | 6902.40 |
| License | 435.00 | Tot Pmts | 28502.40 |
| Total | 26600.00 | Def Pmt | 33502.40 |

60 months @ 475.04

| | | | |
|---|---|---|---|
| Investment | 21600.00 | Amt Fin | 21600.00 |
| Rate/Return | 8.00 | A.P.R. | 11.50 |
| Period (mos.) | 60 | Term (mos.) | 60 |
| Interest | 10580.67 | Fin Chg | 6902.40 |

It costs $3678.27 more to pay cash

### Finance: $0 Down

| | | | |
|---|---|---|---|
| Price | 24135.90 | Down | 0.00 |
| Doc | 35.00 | Rate | 11.50 |
| Tax | 1994.10 | Fin Chg | 8500.00 |
| License | 435.00 | Tot Pmts | 35100.00 |
| Total | 26600.00 | Def Pmt | 35100.00 |

60 months @ 585.00

| | | | |
|---|---|---|---|
| Investment | 26600.00 | Amt Fin | 26600.00 |
| Rate/Return | 8.00 | A.P.R. | 11.50 |
| Period | 60 | Term (mos.) | 60 |
| Interest | 13029.90 | Fin Chg | 8500.00 |

It costs $4529.90 more to pay cash

### Lease: $5000 Down

| | | | |
|---|---|---|---|
| Cap Cost | 24135.90 | Cap Red | 3685.76 |
| Net Cap | 20775.14 | Tax/Red | 304.08 |
| Residual | 12835.50 | License | 435.00 |
| Total Dep | 7939.64 | Sec Dep | 250.00 |
| Bank Fee | 325.00 | 1st. Pmt | 325.16 |
| Factor | 5.00 | Total | 5000.00 |

| | |
|---|---|
| Monthly Dep | 132.33 |
| Monthly Fee | 168.05 |
| 60 months @ | 325.16 |

### Lease: $0 Down

| | | | |
|---|---|---|---|
| Cap Cost | 25280.00 | Cap Red | 0.00 |
| Net Cap | 25605.00 | Tax/Red | 0.00 |
| Residual | 12835.50 | License | 455.00 |
| Total Dep | 12769.50 | Sec Dep | 250.00 |
| Bank Fee | 325.00 | 1st. Pmt | 438.44 |
| Factor | 5.00 | Total | 1143.44 |

(Fees are added back into the Cap Cost)

| | | | |
|---|---|---|---|
| New Cap | 25280.00 | | |
| Old Cap | 24136.00 | | |
| Fees | 1144.00 | 60 months @ | 438.44 |

### Options at the end of the lease term:

If the car is worth more than the residual, trade or sell at a profit.

If the car is worth the residual, buy it or re-finance.

If the car is worth less than the residual, return it to the bank.

Never give the prospect a choice between something and nothing.

Let him choose between something and somethign else.

- Zig Ziglar

## Plan A and Plan B

Once you have the customer interested in discussing payments, a successful technique is to compare two options, usually Leasing vs Financing. Spell out the factors on a sheet of paper, so that your presentation looks like a shorter version of the previous page. Determine whether the customer's primary motive is payment, downpayment, or the features and benefits of each way. Highlight your presentation accordingly.

| **Advantages of Leasing** | **Advantages of Financing** |
|---|---|
| No more sales tax deduction on loans | Own the car outright after term |
| No more interest deduction on loans | Opoortunity to use larger downpayment, reducing debt |
| No more 6% investment credit | Equity position reached sooner |
| Depreciation is longer than 5 years and never total | |
| Lease payments can be expensed monthly for business | |
| A new car every 3 or 4 years | |
| No down payment required | |
| Capital is conserved for investment | |
| Monthly payments are lower | |
| Tax is only paid monthly and there is no obligation to pay 100% of the tax if the vehicle is returned | |
| No risk with a closed-end lease | |
| More car for less money | |

Article in San Jose Mercury News, September 9, 1991

## Chrysler offers new financing

By Janet Braunstein
Knight-Ridder News Service

DETROIT — Finding itself short of new products to sell as the 1992 model year approaches, Chrysler Corp. has come up with some new ways to promote what it has.

And Chrysler's competitors may end up having to follow suit.

Instead of completely redesigned cars and trucks, which won't begin appearing in showrooms until March, Chrysler is offering buyers a new, less-expensive financing, a choice of two warranties, along with a guarantee that its minivans will hold their value as well as its closest competitors.

The new financing, called the Gold Key Plus program, isn't a lease or a conventional car loan. It falls between the two, offering buyers lower monthly payments and a shorter finance term of two to four years.

"I'm sure its competitors will end up offering the exact same program," said Ronald Glantz, analyst with Dean Witter Reynolds in San Francisco.

### How program works

- Buyers pay a minimum down payment of 5 per cent.

- Chrysler determines what the value of the car or truck will be at the end of the term.

- That "fixed value" is subtracted from the selling price. Buyers make payments on the difference.

- The buyer has title to the car. Under a lease, the lease company owns the car.

- At the end of the term, the buyer may keep the car or turn it in. To keep it, the buyer can refinance with the same payments as during the original loan.

The program, offered through Chrysler Credit, should help buyers avoid the 60-month loans that became popular in the 1980's. Those created unhappy customers and high default rates because toward the end, the customer often ends up owing more than the car is worth.

Chrysler hopes it will make it easier for consumers to buy new cars instead of opting for nearly new cars from rental fleets.

Chrysler is touting the choice of warranties it is giving 1992 buyers. Rather than drop its long but limited seven-year, 70,000-mile powertrain warranty, Chrysler will let buyers choose it or substitute a three-year bumper-to-bumper warranty.

To protect its minivan market share, Chrysler is guaranteeing that the resale value of its minivans will remain equal to or better than that of its best-selling competitor at the time of trade-in.

In its 1992 commercials, Chrysler aims at Ford, Chevrolet, Honda, Nissan and Cadillac in comparisons.

This is especially true in truck advertising. Dodge won't get a new full-size pickup until 1994. So for 1992, Dodge is pounding its truck-power advantages in the Dakota and the full-size but aged Ram trucks.

This is a trend that may spread to other captive finance companies. The major banks are generally too conservative for this kind of program. Like any other payment program, success will hinge on the bottom line: term and payment. The conditions under which Chrysler will 'buy back' the vehicle will determine its endurance over time.

## Business Lease

The documentation required to support a business lease has often proved to be a mystery to even the most professional salespeople. The following is routinely stipulated by lessors:

**Business Application:** containing bank references, particularly the name of a business banker.

**Current Financial Statement:** for all but the largest companies, banks will ask for the previous year-end and the current financial statement.

**Personal Application:** for all but the largest companies, banks will require the guarantee of a qualified corporate officer.

**Personal Tax Return:** the guarantor must qualify as if leasing personally.

**Partnership Agreement:** if the company is a partnership, not a corporation.

**Doing Business As:** most banks will allow DBA without further documentation, if the lessee is peronally qualified.

**Corporate Resolution:** this is the bank's own form. The corporate secretary signs the form, authorizing the other corporate officer to sign the lease on behalf of the company.Corporate resolutions must be dated before the date of the lease. A corporate officer who occupies all three positions would sign in both places, authorizing herself to sign. Most banks require the corporate seal on the form.

---

An institution is the lengthened shadow of one man.

- Ralph Waldo Emerson

# Lease Notes

Sales gross is 15% - 20% higher on a lease

Reserve is 15% - 20% higher on a lease

Establish a continuing training program that keeps the sales staff aware of the benefits of leasing

Use Plan A vs Plan B to overcome objections

Use leasing as a closing tool. Don't begin a payment presentation with a lease payment. Save the best for last.

An amortization program is helpful, both for estimating payoffs and reassuring customers.

Sales tax on a lease can be applied in three different areas: tax on the monthly payment, tax on the cap reduction and tax on the residual value, if the vehicle is purchased at the end of the lease.

The complaint heard most often about leasing is "I got ripped off at termination". Those cusotmers turned in a car after three years on a five year term. Shorter lease terms are becoming more popular, especially on lower-priced cars. The dealer sees more customer turn-around and the customer sees more new cars. The lowest payment may not always be the one the customer prefers, once leasing is explained correctly.

Lease payments make great advertising. The following information needs to be disclosed, if actual payment figures are provided:

- a statement that the program advertised is a lease
- the total fees due at signing or a disclosure that no money is required at lease inception
- the schedule, number and amount of periodic payments during the course of the lease and the total of these payments.
- a statement about whether the lessee has the option to purchase the vehicle, at what time and for how much.
- a statement of what liabilities the lessee may incur at the end of the lease.

# Notes

# Notes

# The Cash Deal

*The greatest discovery of my generation is that human beings can alter their lives by altering the attitudes of their minds.*

*- William James*

Very few 'cash' deals are actually cash deals. Often the money is coming from another source. As part of your responsibility to verify payment, when presented with a check, always ask if it is good now. If not, where is the money coming from? If it is coming from another financing source, that is the time to present your case for handling the financing at the dealership.

If it really is all cash, the customer may have decided to buy the car that way in order to avoid the 'hassle' of dealing with finance and the finance manager. When you show him that financing is a simple process, that you are a friend, and that money can be saved, the customer may take your advice. The money the customer is using was probably in an interest-bearing account. What rate if interest was it earning? Now is the opportunity for a cash conversion.

Stay in touch with the current market on Certificates of Deposit (CDs). What are the rates locally? A concrete example gets the most attention. "If you put your money in County Bank down the street, Mr. Customer, here's what you could add to your bottom line in four or five years". Use your clipping file to show current rates.

Those customers who insist on paying cash may also be more sensitive to protecting such a large investment. Packaging your services and offering a cash discount might be timely.

Be careful about taking checks and agreeing to hold them for any length of time. A 'hold' check is legally a promissory note, not cash payment. If you have to hold a check for more than a day or two, you may want to contract the customer as well, just in case. If the customer "just needs to transfer funds", that time is usually allowed during the normal processing of the checks. Be sure that you know where the money is coming from. Never accept a post-dated check, nor a check with a note on it indicating it should be deposited at a later date.

Payment in actual currency is a sensitive issue these days. Federal law states that all cash transactions over $10,000 be reported to the IRS. This reporting must not be discussed with the customer. No customer signature is necessary. If you do discuss the report with the customer, you may be liable as an accomplice if something illegal is going on. The combination of cashier's checks and cash is included under this law. Discuss this potential scenario with the dealer principal and follow his instructions.

# The Cash Deal

- Verify the check whenever possible, unless you know the customer well.

- Obtain a 5-line customer statement (name, address, license number, social security number, birthdate) and run a credit bureau before delivery

- If the funds are provided by a third party, check that person out too.

- Determine the source of the funds. Few people keep large amounts of cash in a checking account.

- Verify insurance. Payment by check is not a complete transaction until the check clears the bank.

- Show the payment in full as a downpayment on the purchase order. The customer's copy is a receipt.

- The occasion of such a large single investment is an opportunity to present a 'long-term protection package'.

- Report any currency transaction over $10,000 to the Internal Revenue Service on form 8300. Do not discuss this reporting with the customer. The customer does not have to sign the form.

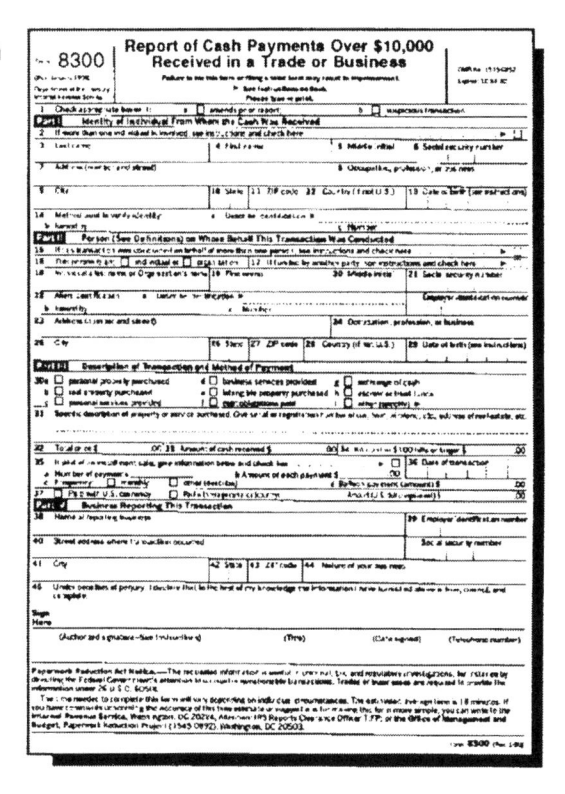

# Selling

> Everyone lives by selling something.
>
> - Robert Louis Stevenson

Selling is a transfer of feeling. If you can get the customer to feel the way you feel about your product or service ... to see things the same way you do ... he or she will buy what you have to offer. When you know your product thoroughly and believe in its value without question, you are already halfway to the sale. The rest is technique. How do you get your experience across to the customer?

## Be an Authority

Selling in the F&I office is a unique situation. You are a manager. You are introduced as an authority. You are the representative of the dealership who will sign the customer's paperwork and make everything legal. This is a strong position from which to sell. Maintain your status as an authority, establish rapport with the customer, gain her trust and you should sell something on virtually every deal. And selling, after all, is what you came to work to do.

Authority is a different concept than Control. Both concepts, however, depend on the perception of the customer. If he sees no need to follow your direction, you have no control. If she doesn't respect what you say, you have no authority. *Control is power taken and authority is power given.* Authority is granted by one to another. Control is usually exercised against another's will. The point is that the customer may *resent* control and *appreciate* authority, especially when his own knowledge is incomplete.

Being an authority also means being authentic. Authentic means unquestionably true. If you have presented a confident, competent and consistent image to the customer, you will appear to be authentic. If the customer senses no contradiction to your expertise and your enthusiasm about your services, she will certify you as a genuine authority.

The other part of being an authority is becoming an author. By doing your selling job correctly, you become the author of your customer's experience. For a little while, you create the world as he or she sees it. Your belief, your conviction and your advice will affect their assumptions about the world. As you will see, perception itself is actually a matter of choices.

> In the province of the mind, what one believes to be true either is true or becomes true.
>
> - John Lilly+

## Be a Counselor

The way to enhance the role that comes with the position of business manager is to take the approach of a counselor. Find out what the customer wants and show him how to get it. The word "persuade" is derived from two Latin words - "per" meaning "through" and "suadere", meaning "to advise". this is an art. We all know that simply "telling" anybody anything does little to change behavior.

Most people buy a car only 5 or 6 times in a lifetime. You deal with automobile purchases every day. You are the professional. You are the expert. The customer is aware of this too. She doesn't want to be intimidated by it. She wants to benefit from your experience. In this chapter are not only some of the techniques used by the best salespeople, but also tools of the best counselors and therapists. Not surprisingly, they are often the same. Adopt the role of advisor. Your customers will apreciate it.

## Be a Psychologist

The modern approach to selling is based on recent studies of how the brain actually works. Psychologists have made great progress in understanding how we think, how we process information and why we make the choices we do.

Each of us, every day, faces a world that provides much more stimulation to the nervous system than the brain can make sense of all at once. For example, the eye alone can process 5 million bits of information per second. the brain can only process 500 bits per second ... and that has to include information about sounds and feelings as well. Somehow a selection procedure must take place.

Biologists have discovered that a part of the brain, called the hippocampus, may perform a 'gating' function. Working through the internal core of the brain stem, this part of the limbic system of the brain 'chooses' from the information available. In this way, the signals that reach the receptors in the nervous system are regulated. Only a small part of the world 'out there' is selected by awareness to be noticed. Otherwise each of us would be totally overwhelmed ... as babies are.

Not only must the brain make choices by selecting from the information available, it must connect that information to what is already stored in memory. This is necessary so that things will 'make sense'. It is a primary function of the brain to connect individual moments in time. It does this by acting like a computer, placing a pattern on an event so that it can be understood.

The Complete F&I Reference Book

To the eyes of a miser a guinea is far more beautiful than the sun, and a bag worn with money has more beautiful proportions than a vine filled with grapes.

The tree which moves some to tears of Joy is in the eyes of others only a green thing which stands in the way.

As a man is,
so he sees.

- William Blake

Look at the picture of the triangle. Do you see a white triangle, pointing downward? Think carefully. Where is that triangle? The answer is that the white triangle is in your mind. It is the way that your brain has 'made sense' of the information presented.

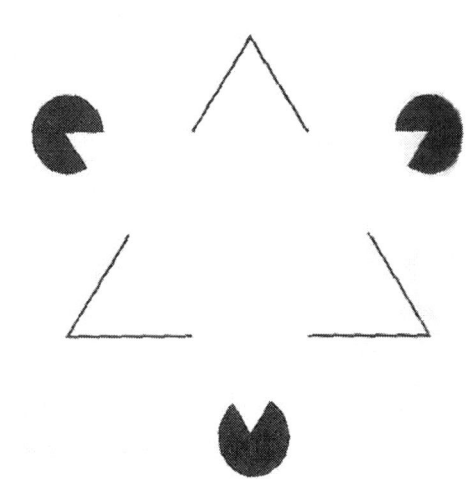

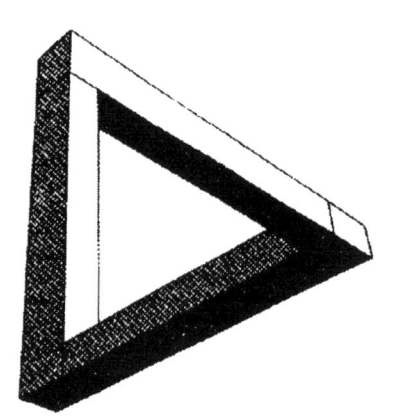

Look at the triangle on the left. As you look, you can almost feel your brain trying to make sense out of the information from the eyes. It wants to impose a pattern onto the information, realized from previous experience ... and it's not possible.

As you look at the steps, you can feel your mind trying to perceive a pattern that isn't there. Your attention seems to spin in a loop.

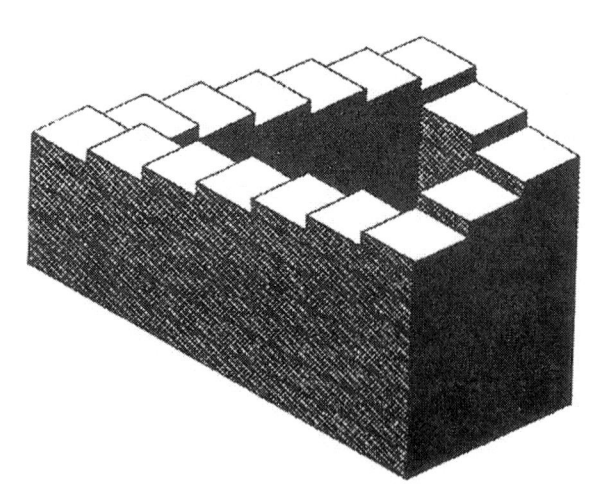

> Sorcerers say that we are inside a bubble.
>
> It is a bubble into which we are placed at the moment of our birth. At first the bubble is open, but then it begins to close until it has sealed us in.
>
> That bubble is our perception. We live inside that bubble all of our lives. And what we witness on its round walls is our own reflection.
>
> - Carlos Castenada

What we see is determined by what we are looking for. Some neuro-psychologists call these patterns we would impose on our environment 'Plans'. If you are operating from a Plan that says "All dogs are messy and dirty", what's the first thing you see when a dog crosses your path? Another word for a Plan is a State. If you are in a particularly happy state, for instance, you will see the world through "rose-colored glasses". If your state changes, you will see things "in a different light". Your motive, your Plan, your state of mind at any given time determines not only what information you will perceive but also what that information *means*.

Looking at the picture on the right, most people will see a sketch of an old woman. She has a jarge, crooked nose and a pointed chin. She is looking down. She has a shawl over her head and a feather rising from her hair. there is another picture there.
Can you see it?

There is, in that information, also a sketch of a young woman. She is turning away. Her nose is barely visible and you can only see what would be her left eyelash. What is a thin mouth for the old woman is a necklace for the young woman. The line around a nostril for the old woman is the young woman's jaw line. Both are wearing a heavy black coat. Once you learn to see both the old woman and the young woman, you will notice a curious development. You cannot see both at the same time. As you try, you will feel your mind re-organizing the information. What you see depends on your 'frame of mind'.

Looking left, do you see a large ceremonial cup ... a chalice ... or two people facing each other? Acting like a psychologist means seeing things from the customer's point of view. *Then* you can lead the customer to see things another way. In sales, the big mistake is to *disagree* with the customer, assuming that they just don't see the light. The point is that there is more than one light. To obtain a customer's agreement, see things his or her way first.

Desire engenders belief.

- Marcel Proust

## Feature the appropriate benefits.

When you see that a customer has a Plan to be as safe and secure as possible, show her how to protect herself against potentially devastating loss. When you see that a customer's priority is an eye-catching image, a lease might enable him to drive a car more suitable to his Plan ... perhaps adding a couple of striking accessories. Someone whose priority is time management and efficiency won't want to run all over town doing paperwork. Often the customer is simply running a program that says "Don't trust car dealers". Agree with their apprehension and show them they can trust you.

## Context makes meaning.

What it is depends on how, when and where we see it. Looking at the graphic on the right, what is the symbol in the middle of those letters and numbers? Below, which line is longer?

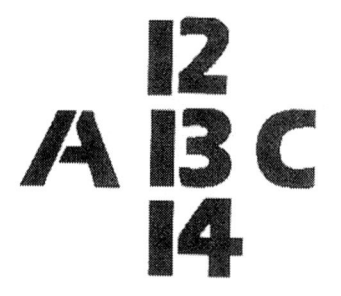

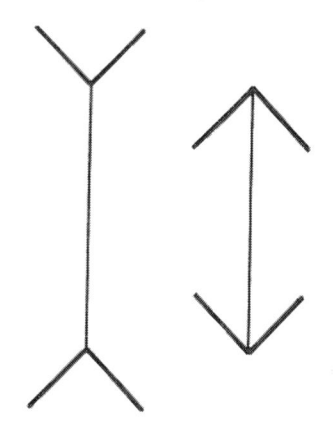

Since we know that people perceive information only in the light of their intentions and expectations, we could say that, in the deepest sense, the context is always the mind of the person who is looking. But the brain automatically sorts with other clues as well.

The 500 most commonly used words in the Oxford English Dictionary have 14070 different meanings. Like the word 'Love. In life, it means everything. In tennis, it means nothing. Have you noticed that when you are in the market for (engaged in a Plan to buy) a new Toyota, all you see on the road are Toyotas? Whether you are short or tall depends on who you are standing next to. A good deal is one that is better than the last one.

The context of your dealership and your office determine whether you are perceived as a professional. The context of your relationship with your customer will determine how you personally are perceievd. It is not actually *what* is happening around us that makes our experience. It is how we *perceive* what is happening that counts.

> You see what you want to see,
> and you hear
> what you want to hear.
>
> - The Rock Man

## Summary

Have you ever taken a test for color blindness? If you don't see red, does it mean that red isn't there? Another example is the sound of your own voice. When you hear the sound of your own voice played back on a recording, you are ... for a moment ... convinced it's not you. It has to be you though, because everyone else recognizes it.

The reason that you don't recognize the sound of your own voice is that your experience of your own voice is internal ... sound resonating through bone. Everyone else has always heard your voice the way that you did from the recording ... pressure waves moving through the air.

The same is true of all our senses. For each of us, the world can only be what we experience it to be. Things mean only what they mean to each person. What is meaningful to one, may not be meaningful to another. This is why people like people who see things the same way they do. It is a confirmation of reality. And it's why attitude is so important.

Seeing, listening and feeling are not the simple, passive processes that we imagine them to be. Objective information about the outside world does not just flow into a waiting mind. Perception itself is a learned, interactive activity. The mind and brain combine new information collected by the nervous system with information from previous experience and current beliefs to construct an on-going image of the world. The brain works from Plans to organize the information so that it 'makes sense'. Once a Plan is in place, it will determine the value of the incoming data and structure *things* accordingly.

Next we will look more carefully at how to discover the Plans ... expectations, intentions and states ... and how to relate to them. There are techniques with which to establish customer rapport ... that is be in agreement with his or her state ... and ways to present your products and services in the customers' terms. The customer wants to benefit from your experience, since you are perceived as an authority and a counselor who has her best interests at heart. By following this approach, you create the selling process as a Win-Win situation.

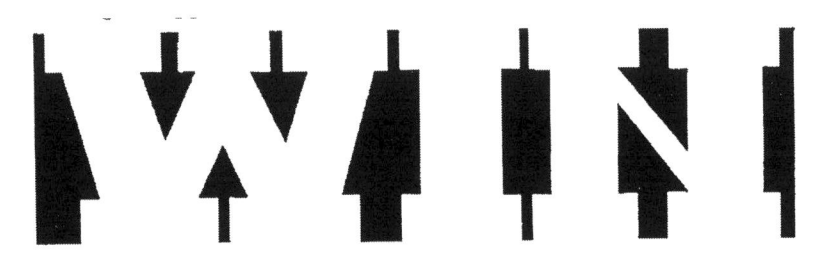

## Neuro-Linguistic Programming

A person acts as a result of the Plan from which he or she is operating. Another way to say that is that actions result from particular states. A state is created by the way we re-present the world to ourselves. People process information primarily in three ways: sight, sound and feeling. Each of us emphasizes one particular way. 'Visual' customers like to be shown. They prefer to 'see for themselves' ... pictures, graphs and tables. Those customers who go more by how something 'sounds' will be more affected by the conviction and sincerity in your voice. Suggestions literally 'sound' good or bad to them. People who are primarily emotional will make choices on the basis of what 'feels right' to them.

The key to establishing rapport is to understand how each person is presenting the world 'out there' to themselves. We have choices about how we perceive things. What is the customer's primary mode of processing? Once we know that, we can 'speak their language'.

We talk in the same language that we think. Visual people will use visual terms:

> "I don't see the point in leasing"
> "I see myself keeping the car for a long time"
> "I like the way the car looks"
> "Let me make this perfectly clear"

People who process primarily in the sound mode will say:

> "I heard that leasing is not a good idea"
> "I have talked myself into holding on to my old car"
> "Everybody said this is the car to buy"
> "Listen carefully"

Emotional people will express themselves in 'feeling' language:

> "Leasing just doesn't feel right"
> "I'm going to hold on to my old car"
> "I like the way this car handles"
> "Follow me closely on this"

By the words the customer chooses, he is telling you how he wants to get the point you wish to make.

---

*Words are, of course, the most powerful drug used by mankind.*

*- Rudyard Kipling*

Here is a table of the three representational systems and how they appear on the human face. the eyes show which system the person is accessing, since eye movements are not under voluntary control. for the 10%-15% of the population that is left-handed, the directions are reversed.

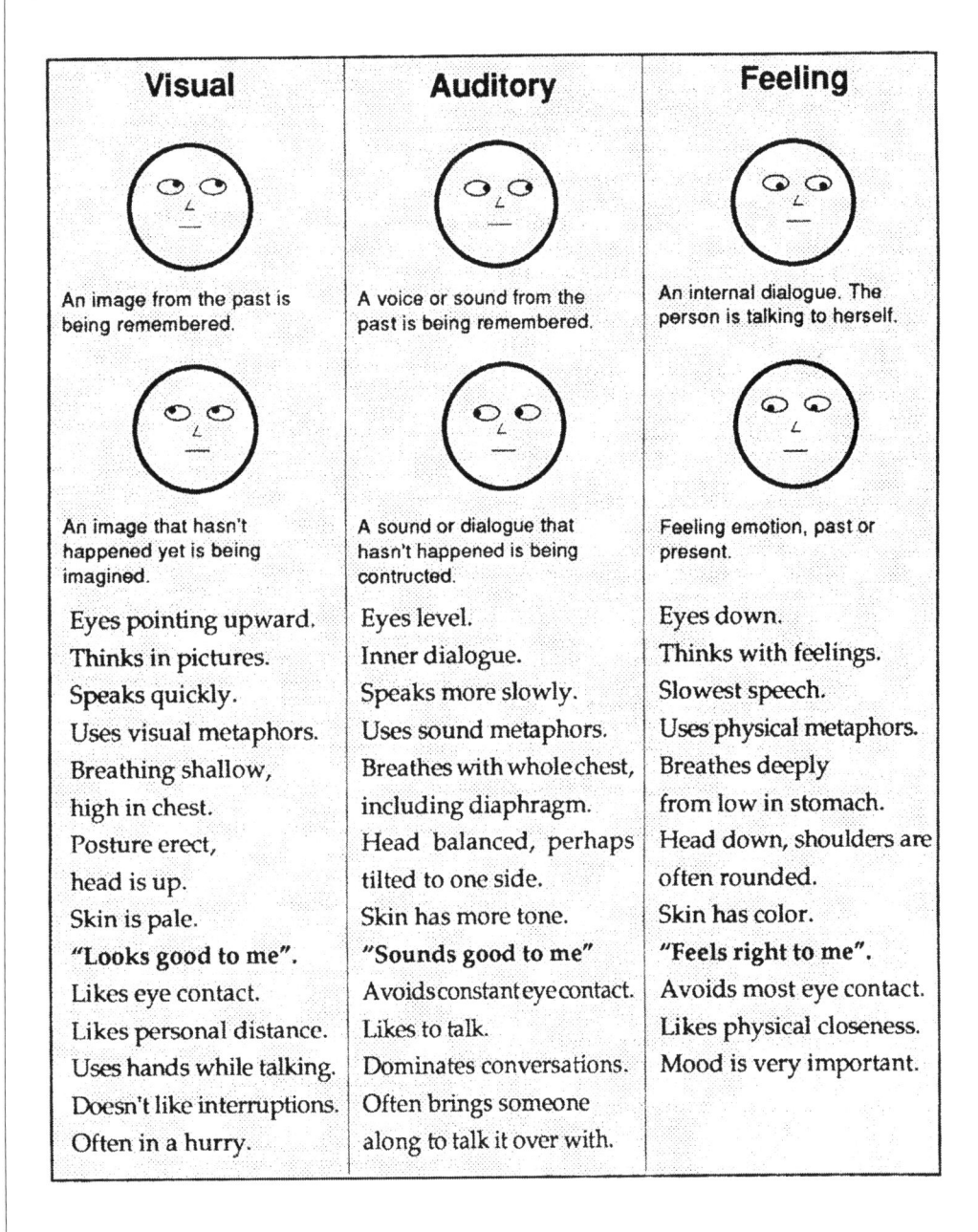

> It is a point of cunning, to wait upon him with whom you speak, with your eyes; as the Jesuits give it in precept; for there be many wise men that have secret hearts and transparent countenances.
>
> - Francis Bacon

| Visual | Auditory | Feeling |
|---|---|---|
| An image from the past is being remembered. | A voice or sound from the past is being remembered. | An internal dialogue. The person is talking to herself. |
| An image that hasn't happened yet is being imagined. | A sound or dialogue that hasn't happened is being contructed. | Feeling emotion, past or present. |
| Eyes pointing upward. Thinks in pictures. Speaks quickly. Uses visual metaphors. Breathing shallow, high in chest. Posture erect, head is up. Skin is pale. "Looks good to me". Likes eye contact. Likes personal distance. Uses hands while talking. Doesn't like interruptions. Often in a hurry. | Eyes level. Inner dialogue. Speaks more slowly. Uses sound metaphors. Breathes with whole chest, including diaphragm. Head balanced, perhaps tilted to one side. Skin has more tone. "Sounds good to me" Avoids constant eye contact. Likes to talk. Dominates conversations. Often brings someone along to talk it over with. | Eyes down. Thinks with feelings. Slowest speech. Uses physical metaphors. Breathes deeply from low in stomach. Head down, shoulders are often rounded. Skin has color. "Feels right to me". Avoids most eye contact. Likes physical closeness. Mood is very important. |

The purpose in observing where the customer is 'coming from' is only to be able to reflect the same behavior back. what the behavior 'means' doesn't matter.

## Mirroring

People like people who are like themselves. To build rapport, use the same representational system that the customer is using. In reply to the visual customer, use visual terms:

> "I can see what you mean..."
> "I can picture that."
> "It's very clear to me that ..."

Show the **visual** customer pictures or other display material. Create visual images of your services:

> "Picture yourself five years from now, pulling into the line
> on a Service Department driveway at a dealership.
> It's been a long, hot day and the mechanic shows you
> an air-conditioning unit on your car that's leaking.
> What labor rates can you imagine are posted on the wall?
> What do you see as the price of parts?"

Or

> "Financing instead of paying cash looks like money in the bank to me."

The **auditory** customer wants to know that she is being heard:

> "I hear what you are saying about gas prices these days ...."
> "Sounds to me like you are a careful person"
> "Does that ring a bell with you?"

This customer wants the facts. Give him numbers and figures ... the more information, the better. Use your voice tone and inflection deliberately. Tell him a personal story. Begin with "Listen to this ...".

> "I recently had an experience that taught me to listen
> to my better judgement. Four years ago, I could have bought
> a service contract for half of what they cost now.
> Because I didn't have one, I ignored a 'ping'
> in my engine until last month. It cost me $1400."

---

*As we think, so we speak; as we speak, so we think.*

- Lister Sinclair

When responding to customers who navigate primarily in the **'feeling'** mode, use expression that match:

> "I get that feeling too"
> "That really touches me because ...."
> "I get a sense that ...."

Speak from the heart and put emotion into the words you use. Share your feelings:

> "Wouldn't you feel better knowing that if, God forbid, something should happen to you, your spouse could carry on without your income. She could get her hands on the title right away and the car would not be tied up in probate."

Rapport is further enhanced by mirroring other patterns produced by the other person. Don't mimic, but make similar movements, with similar timing. Mirror the position of the head and the arms, the breathing pattern and the tone of voice. Join the customer where he is, so that you can lead him to where you want him to be. Studies show that brainwaves actually do synchronize between people who establish rapport. People are more likely to trust those who interpret the world the same way as themselves. People do not trust others who 'see things' differently.

## State of mind

A person's state of mind determines how he or she will see the world. As a salesperson, the first thing you want to do is make sure that the customer is in a relaxed and receptive state of mind. State determines behavior. It is a very common sales mistake to present a product or service and then try to get the customer to feel good about it. Working the other way around is much more effective. The order in which events occur affects their meaning.

Use the first few minutes of your meeting with the customer, not only to confirm your authority, but also to establish common ground. While talking with him about the weather, current events or his new car, you are observing his body language and the kinds of words he uses. Reflecting that behavior back to him builds rapport and produces a more receptive state. In NLP, this is called constructing an agreement frame. You and the customer not only have some of the same experiences in common, you appear to look at the world the same way. Suggestions presented in this light are much more likely to continue to find agreement.

---

*It ain't nothin' till I call it.*

- Bill Klem
Professional Baseball Umpire

> We all, in one way or another, send our little messages to the world ...
>
> And rarely do we send our messages consciously. We act out our state of being with nonverbal body language.
>
> We lift one eye for relief, We rub our noses for puzzlement. We clasp our arms to isolate ourselves or protect ourselves.
>
> We shrug our shoulders for indifference, wink one eye for intimacy, tap our fingers for impatience, slap our foreheads for forgetfulness.
>
> The gestures are numerous and while some are deliberate ... there are some, such as rubbing our noses for puzzlement, or clasping our arms to protect ourselves, that are mostly unconscious.
>
> - Julius Fast
> Body Language

## Use body language

Only 7% of our communication is actually in the words we use. 38% of communication is in the tone of voice and 55% is through our body language. Most people trust their visual information more than the other senses. There are many books written exclusively about body language. Be conscious of what you are communicating with your hands, your posture, your facial expression, your timing and so on. Even the physical distance between you and the customer sends a message. 'Visual' people prefer a little distance, so that they can see you. 'Feeling' people like to be close enough to touch.

Eyes are very important, as we all know. There is a time when eye contact can be threatening and a time when eye contact is essential. Take your cue from the customer. Does she want 'to look you in the eye"? Facial expressions are our main source of visual information. Some studies have shown that we are born to recognize a smiling face ... so smiling is obviously significant. Become aware of your expressions. Gain control of them. For clues about appropriate behavior, look to the customer. The best salespeople are also good actors.

## Use you voice

Lately, videotaping a salesperson's presentation and playing it back to him or her has become a popular training method. These sessions reveal that salespeople speak in a monotone much more often than they are aware of. English is a language of inflection. *The way you say something determines what it means.* Repeat to yourself some of the lines you use most often. Is there a way you can add effectiveness by emphasizing a particular word? Plan to change your tone of voice during your presentation. How or when should you do this? Take your cue from the customer. Are they happy or sad? They should probably sound nervous. Do they? Are they loud or can you barely hear what is being said? Are they making statements or asking questions? Are they talking *to* you, or *about* themselves?

An excellent way to gain rapport is to use a counselling technique known as 'active listening'. Listen. Then say to the other person, "Just to be sure I understand you, you said ...". Repeat back to the customer the exact same words, in the same order and in the same tone of voice. When a customer agrees that you have heard him correctly, he will often go on to sell himself. Don't try to sell at that point. Just listen and agree.

> How well we communicate is determined not by how well we say things but by how well we are understood.
>
> - Andrew Grove
> CEO Intel Corporation

## Use the right words

When you are making presentations, use words that appeal to the imagination ... words that paint pictures, tell stories and speak to feelings and fantasies. These would be words that are heard on the right side of the brain.

Don't say, "What if your car breaks down?"

Say: "Imagine that the car developed a leak in a faulty head gasket and hot oil burst through, soaking the entire engine. Wouldn't you feel relieved to know all the damage resulting from that explosion would be covered?"

Once you have set the stage (the agreement frame), you must connect that state to the need for your services in order to close the sale. Connecting words play a role at this point.

## Connecting Words

The one word that is the nemesis of most salespeople is "but". This word negates any statement that goes before it. Changing the word "but" to the word "and" keeps the conversation going in one direction and maintains agreement.

The customer says: "Leasing sounds like a good idea, *but* it's not for me"

You reply:

"I hear you saying, Mr. Customer, that leasing is a good idea *and* it's not for you. If it is such a good idea, what is it about leasing that doesn't fit into your plans?"

The customer says, "The service contract is a good idea *but* I can't afford it".

You reply: "You say that the service contract is a good idea *and* you can't afford it. Then if it were affordable, would you like to include it?"

> Men willingly believe what they wish.
>
> - Julius Caesar

The customer says, "I'd like to keep my cash, *but* I don't like to pay interest".

You reply: "You would like to keep your cash *and* you don't like to pay interest. What if interest were paid to you?"

The change from 'but' to 'and' can be quite productive.

Another pair of words to inter-change is 'If' and 'When'. Look at the difference between:

"*If* you finance instead of paaying cash, the compound interest that you gain from investing is greater than the interest you pay for the loan"

and

"*When* you finance instead of paying cash, the compound interest that you gain from investing is greater than the interest that pay for the loan"

"Since" and "As" are also connecting words:

"*Since* you obviously understand the value of insurance, you must consider this deal."

"*As* you have probably noticed, this is something that I believe in".

Connecting words maintain the agreement frame. Connect a true statement to a selling statement:

"*Since* you are going to be keeping the car for a long time, you might want to consider the need for long term protection against the rising cost of repair."

This process ... maintaining the agreement frame, is something we do unconsciously all the time:

"I can relate to that ... Exactly ... I can appreciate that ... You're right ... I can understand that ... I agree ... I respect tthat ...."

Just add a connecting word. Each connection leads along the path to purchase.

## Use embedded commands

Studies in marketing and applied behavioral science have found that we respond unconsciously to 'command' statements. Many finance managers have a story about how they finally just told the customer to "Sign it. Everything will be OK". And the customer signed.

To go a step further, and perhaps be a little more subtle with the technique, place the commands within the context of your conversation. In NLP, these are called embedded commands. When discussing the advisability of financing the car, you might say, "Put $5000 down and your payment is only $300 a month". The statement does not have to *sound* like a command. It is the structure of the statement that works.

> "Include the service contract in your lease and your payment is only $10 more a month".

On a subsconscious level, the brain is very literal. That is why Neuro-Linguistic Programming works. You will remember that commands were some of the first words we learned as children.

## Use the customer's name

The other first words we learned were names, especially our own. Make a habit of looking down at the paperwork to recall the customer's name. Let your instinct tell you if you should be formal and use the last name, or more casual, using the first name. This is particularly important when you have two or more customers in front of you and you want to keep everyone's attention.

## Reframe an objection

What someone perceives depends on what frame of reference they are using. For example, no one needs a service contract when they buy a car. The car comes with a factory warranty and new cars are not supposed to break down. You can align yourself with a customer who says she doesn't need it. Right now. You can agree with that. Then you can re-frame her point of view. Look at the same need five years from now. Look at the cost in the context of seven years of coverage. What will parts cost five years from now? How about labor? In a different context, things look different.

---

When firmness is sufficient, harshness is unnecessary.

- Napoleon Bonaparte

> The toughest thing about success is that you've got to keep on being a success.
>
> Talent is only a starting point in business. you've got to keep working that talent.
>
> - Irving Berlin

"I don't need credit insurance. I'm healthy".

becomes

"No one needs insurance when they're healthy, Mr. Customer. You're in a fairly high risk occupation though. What would happen if you couldn't work for a while?"

Or  "I always like to own my cars" (lease objection)

becomes

"I understand that Mr. Customer. Who actually owned that last car you financed? Was there a lienholder?"

**Handling objections**

Welcome objections. You come to work to sell. Objections give you the opportunity to do that. An objection is an expression of interest on the part of the customer. If he wasn't interested, he wouldn't bother to object. With an objection, the customer is showing you his point of view. Join him at that point and lead him to see things your way. Sometimes you can answer objections by anticipating them. Sometimes you will respond directly with information the customer simply didn't have. Occasionally, you will settle for lowering the significance of an objection, since the customer seems determined to win a point. Once in a while, you may ignore an objection completely.

What is important to remember is that you believe in the services you are offering. It should be clear to customers that you want them to see the reason for buying. There is no need to be defensive. When the customer offers an objection, she wants to see what you will do. It is an opportunity to show the depth of your sincerity and the extent of your enthusiasm. In many studies of sales situations, it is found that the customer wants to buy ... if you will only give her a reason. With an objection, the customer is actually asking for that reason.

> What we see, then, may be considered a nervous response to what we look at.
>
> - Colin Cherry
> On Human Communication

- ❖ Anticipate the most common objections. For example, a customer buying a car with a four-year factory warranty is likely to say that the factory coverage is enough. Anticipate this by asking "Do you plan to keep the car longer than four years?" early on in the conversation.

- ❖ Maintain the agreement frame. Acknowledge the customers' point of view. Show how their concern can be addressed by a benefit you have to offer.

- ❖ An objection can show you what your customer really wants ... what her priorities are.

- ❖ Postpone a price objection until you have had time to establish value.

- ❖ Rephrase and 'soften' an objection. "I hate service contracts" becomes "I understand that you have had a problem with a service contract in the past".

- ❖ Don't 'over-answer' an objection. Make your point and stop.

- ❖ Be sure you are dealing with a decision-maker. Otherwise you can answer objections all day long and not close a deal.

- ❖ Use the word 'and' instead of the word 'but'.

- ❖ Never argue with a customer.

- ❖ Listen to the objection. Restate it as a question. "I always pay cash" becomes "You are saying that you don't see the benefit in financing the car?"

- ❖ Isolate the objection. "Is that the only reason you won't lease the car today?"

- ❖ Answer the objection. Convey your feelings and your point of view, then ask the customer to see it your way.

- ❖ Use the objection as a reason to buy. After all, you have determined that the objection was the only obstacle to closing the deal.

- ❖ When the objection is a matter of price, you must either raise the customer's perception of the value or lower his perception of the cost. Before you do, ask "if the price were right, would you buy today?"

- ❖ Don't take objections personally.

- ❖ You don't have to answer all objections. You only need to tip the balance in your direction.

*Tell me,
how did you love my picture?*

*- Samuel Goldwyn*

## Ask Questions

People prefer talking to listening. When you ask questions, customers answer them and become more involved in the relationship you are developing. You are making the customer part of the process. Asking questions reveals the customer's plans and priorities. For example, "Why did you choose this particular car?" Questions will evoke pleasant or unpleasant pictures, sounds or feelings that you want the customer to re-experience. "Remember your first car? What was it about that car?"

The more the customer talks and you consciously work at establishing rapport, the more likely a sale becomes. In your role as counselor, you want to understand the cusotmer's specific situation, so that you can best serve her needs.

"Do you plan to use the car every day?"
"What are your plans for the car?"
"Do you take many long trips?"
"Do you plan on keeping the car for a long time?"
"Are you going to put a lot of miles on the car?"

Other questions may lead to a trial close:

"Are you interested in building your credit rating?"
"Is saving money important to you?"

Follow-up questions encourage the other person to talk:

"What happened then?"
"Why did you do that?"
"How do you feel about that?"
"How does that sound?"

A key question is "Do you plan to keep the car for a long time?" This leads to concern about protecting the investment. By the time you begin your presentation, you have established your role as an expert. You have created rapport. You have defined the need before you offered the solution. Your services are perceived as good advice. At this point, the customer should have questions for you. "Is it better to finance or lease?" "Are these service contracts really any good?" Why should I pay extra for credit insurance?" Of course, the question you hear most is, "How much does it cost?"

## Ask more questions

When you have value statements to make about your products and services, turning them into questions involves your customer:

> "It would feel re-assuring to know your trip would not be interrupted, wouldn't it?"

> "You want the car to look sparkling brand new five years from now, don't you?"

> "These days, the feeling of security that comes with cash in the bank is much more important, isn't it?"

Trial closes can be stated in terms of choices:

> "If you were to finance this car, would you go 48 or 60 months?"

> "If you didn't pay cash, would you finance or lease?"

> "If you were to lease the car, would you prefer normal fees or nothing down?"

> "If you were to consider a service contract, which would be more important, time or miles?"

> "If you were to include insurance, would you prefer life or disability coverage?"

## Believe in what you are doing

The power of belief can slow heart rates and heal wounds. Whether you are aware of it or not, it is your belief that the world is out there that makes it so. It is your belief that makes it the *kind* of world you think it is. Customers buy from salespeople who appear certain about what they are saying. Your belief will sell for you.

---

*There's nothing either good or bad, but thinking makes it so.*

- William Shalespeare

Every great and commanding moment in the annals of the world is the triumph of some enthusiasm.

- Ralph Waldo Emerson

## Use Models

The art and science of Neuro-Linguistic Programming (NLP) was developed in the late 1970's by two authors who began by making a study of the most successful therapists in the world. Why were these particular people so successful, when others who had the same training did not produce such remarkable results? Rather than deal in theory, Richard Bandler and John Grinder noted everything these counselors were saying and doing. Then, to be successful themselves, all they did was copy the behavior. This process is called modelling. It is a powerful learning process that seems to be built into the brain. It is, in fact, how we learn to do most of the things we do. We will copy the language, behavior and beliefs of someone who is in a position we aspire to. We see that it works, so we do it again.

Many of the best salespeople can't tell you exactly why what they do works, but they know it does. The odds are that they are behaving much as described above without being aware of it. Great salespeople naturally involve the customer in the process by asking questions.

> Man is what he believes.
>
> - Anton Chekov

## Great salespeople do the following:

- Sell to everyone you see. No exceptions.

- Don't sell products. Sell what products do and how they make people feel.

- Agree, don't argue. Align yourself with the customer and go from there.

- See the buying situation from the customer's point of view.

- Expect to sell. Your belief determines the outcome.

- Show genuine interest in the customer and his needs. Sincerity sells.

- Establish rapport. Match the other person's manner, tone and timing.

- Find the problem that your product or service will solve.

- Be flexible. People have different motives and needs.

- Be enthusiastic. Act as if you can't believe someone would not want what you have to offer.

- Take responsibility for communication. It's up to you to transfer your feeling about what you have to offer.

- Always ask for the sale. Make buying easier for the customer.

- Establish value before you discuss price.

- Hold back a feature or benefit to close the deal. The service contrac is transferable; the loan has no penalty for early payoff; the alarm also has a remote panic switch; today only there's a discount. Give the customer a reason to change his mind.

- Communicate that you care. Is the name on the Report of Sale the way the customer wants it? Is the payment due on a convenient date? Compliment her on the choice of model or color. Remind her not to rely onthe 'grace' period for insurance coverage, in case there is a claim.

# Notes

# Notes

# Service Contracts

*If we had to point to one single notion which is calculated to damage our industrial performance, to prevent us from competing effectively in the world and ultimately to undermine the basis of a free and diverse society, it is the idea that profit is somehow wrong.*

*- Margaret Thatcher*

Service contracts are usually the second highest source of income to a good F&I department, after financing. It is possible to install a self-insured service contract program. There are companies that will handle the administration for you. There are tax advantages to this, however, these days few dealers welcome the exposure to liability. It is less profitable, but also less risky, to sign up with a service contract company who are themselves insured.

Motivational studies reveal that the fear of loss is a higher priority than the desire for gain. Although most new cars now come with longer factory warranties, buyers are keeping those cars longer. This trend toward the long term inclines the customer to protect the investment. Some aspects of the future are indeed predictable. Prices will rise, inflation is a fact of life, the cost of labor always rises, and cars do sometimes break down. The customer is spending a lot of money for a car they plan to use for a long time. Some reassurance is called for.

The usual objection to a service contract is not that they aren't practical, but that they may not be worth paying a lot of money for ... that one might be better off 'taking a chance' that there will be no problems. Certainly, one of the reasons the customer chose that particular car was for its reliability. In circumstances where the customer sees both sides of the equation, it is *your* belief, *your* enthusiasm, *your* sincerity that will make the difference.

This same attitude should extend to pricing. It is more true with service contracts than any other product that 'gross is just a state of mind'. Consumers are used to paying high prices (comparatively) for service contracts on washers, dryers, refrigerators and stereos. Set the price high enough to allow for discounting in special situations but be consistent. Don't charge more than the stated price and don't discount without a reason.

You should be thoroughly familiar with the service contract program you offer. Ask questions of the representative. Talk with your service manager. Collect a story or two about the efficient handling of claims. Know what makes your program different from other programs the customer may have experienced. As with everything else, know your stuff. Be the expert. If the customer does end up keeping the car for a long time, he or she will be glad they took your advice.

Prime Minister Gladstone speaks to me as if I were a public meeting.

- Queen Victoria

- ❖ Stay consistent with price for each type of service contract. If you discount, do so only with a reason ... cash ... end of month ... beginning of month....

- ❖ Bring information from your conversation back into your presentation. Perhaps the trade has high miles or recent repair ... maybe the customer travels often ... maybe he kept his last car for 10 years.

- ❖ Do not make presentations *at* your customer. Make them *for* your customer. Get her to ask you questions.

- ❖ Relate a personal experience of a need for a service contract.

- ❖ "Do you plan to have the car for a long time?" The customer is paying in today's dollars for whatever retail cost on repair will be 6 or 7 years from now.

- ❖ Remind your customer how much the cost of repairs has risen in the last 4 years. What if that rate of increase continues?

- ❖ Use a waiver form. In case there is a problem later, document that the servic contract was offfered and dclined.

- ❖ Offer a choice of two plans at different prices. For example, offer 7 year/100,000 mile coverage or 7 year/75,000 mile coverage ... with or without a deductible.

- ❖ If the service contract company is re-insured with a major carrier (Prudential, Lloyd's of London ...), point that out to the customer.

- ❖ When possible, break down the cost of the plan to a monthly payment increase ... dollars per year or cents per day.

- ❖ Avoid the 'Bumper to Bumper' type of contracts. The customer wants to see what she is buying.

- ❖ Establish a follow-up program, using information from the service department as well as your own log. Who is nearing the end of their factory warranty? Send a notice to everybody. Those who already have a service contract will ignore your contact. Follow up with a phone call.

- ❖ Enlist service writers in the service drive to help sell. Make sure they are fully informed as to what is available. Ask each of them what it would take to get them to sell 5 contracts a month.

- ❖ Cosigners should always make sure the car is protected.

> Nothing ever succeeds which exuberant spirits have not helped to produce.
>
> - Nietsche

## Presentation

Begin to talk about the service contract after you know how the customer is going to pay for the car. Ask if the salesperson explained the factory warranty that comes with the car. Explain the factory warranty, if the salesperson did not. Tell the customer that the factory warranty may be fine if he only plans to keep the car for a short period of time. Ask the customer if he plans to keep the car for a while? If the customer is absolutely adamant that she will only be keeping the car for a short time, explain the more immmediate benefits of the extended service contract:

- ❖ It is good anywhere in the USA or Canada. If the customer happened to be travelling at the time a problem occurred, there may not be a factory dealer for hundreds of miles.

- ❖ The policy covers a rental car and towing.

- ❖ It is transferable. If the customer offers the car for sale (rather than trading in next time), including a 4 or 5 year repair guantee might help.

- ❖ A pro-rated refund is available. If the customer did trade in the car, she would only pay for the coverage used.

Most customers will indicate that they plan to keep the car for a long time.

> "In that case Mrs. Customer, I strongly recommend the 7 year/100,000 mile coverage. I don't see how you can lose. If you keep the car for seven years, and you have only one repair ... a water pump, for example ... it's bound to cost you twice what it does now. The service contract will always pay retail prices on parts and labor, whatever those prices happen to be six or seven years from now ... wherever you may take the car.
>
> On the other hand, if you offer the car for sale 3 or 4 years from now, you can offer it with a 3 or four year warranty. That will definitely help you sell the car and you will probably get your money back."

> Winning isn't everything, but wanting to win is.
>
> - Vince Lombardi

If you have sold the customer on the concept, he will probably ask, "What does it cover?" If for some strange reason this question is not asked, explain that coverage is extensive. In either event, place the disclosure page of the policy in front of the customer and point to each section of the covered components with your pen. Read aloud, showing just how extensive the coverage is.

Obviously, you want to lead the customer to the question, "How much does it cost?" By this time, you have sold the value. Don't approach the cost until the customer sees that this might be something worthwhile. Quote the cost in terms of monthly payment if possible. If it has to be cash, be firm about the price. You might be the gauge the customer is using to determine value.

Relate a personal experience of a need for a service contract. We have all had one. Even if the customer is already sold, you are reinforcing his good judgement. Save a closer to use, just in case. A zero deductible. Tire damage protection. Always offer alternatives. What if you could provide the longer coverage for the shorter term price?

Be sure any deductible is disclosed. If a waiver is signed, schedule a follow-up.

## Objections

> The average sale is made after the propect has said "No" six times.
>
> - Jeffrey Davidson
> Marketing Consultant

**"It's a new car and it shouldn't break down."**
Agree with the customer. Point out that an automobile has approximately 15,000 moving parts. All it takes is for one part to go wrong ... five years from now ... when the cost of repair is twice as much. Compare the 'internal' coverage to the 'external' coverage on the vehicle - comprehensive and collision insurance. An accident or theft is less likely to happen but more expensive to insure against.

**"I will only put a few thousand miles on the car".**
All the more reason to cover the car with a service contract. Low miles on the car means that the time element will be the deciding factor on term. Five or six years from now, what will it cost to fix an air-conditioner or replace a water pump? If you offer the car for sale, it can come with a repair guarantee.

**"I trade my cars in every couple of years."**
A nice situation to be in. History shows, however, that the customer could probably make more money by retailing the car personally, rather than trading in for a wholesale price. Because of the steadily rising prices of new cars, the used car market is very strong ... especially for a 2 or 3 year-old car with a guarantee against the cost of future repairs. In the meantime, the customer has coverage that will pay the factory deductible, if there is one, and provide for a rental car ... which factory warranties generally don't. If the customer has to offer the car as a trade, there is always a pro-rated refund.

**"I have a friend who is a mechanic."**
The customer is fortunate. Does the friend have access to factory testing equipment? Can the friend get parts free of charge? If the friend is licensed to make repairs, then parts can be obtained under the service contract. Will the friend lend the customer a car to drive? the service contract guarantees substitute transportation. The friend can service the vehicle, under factory guidelines, without voiding the contract.

> The secret of success is constancy to purpose.
>
> - Benjamin Disraeli

### "I will put 40,000 miles on the car in the first year."

All the more reason to cover the car with a service contract, since the factory warranty will expire that much sooner. Obviously, a car is very important to this customer, so the availability of a free rental car should mean something. Claim handling is quick and easy. Out-of-state claims can be handled with a credit card number from the administrator (depending on the program). This customer should always have a service contract to protect the resale value of a car with higher than normal miles.

### "It's not worth the money"

If you don't use it at all, you can still transfer it when you offer your car for sale. You will at least get your money back and it will help you sell the car. If you use it just once, 4 ...5...6 years from now, it will probably pay for itself. If you trade the car in, you can receive a pro-rated refund. You only pay for what you use.

### "It's too expensive"

Now it's just a matter of price. The customer does not yet appreciate the value. Compare the slight increase in monthly payment to the increase of the value of the car at resale, when it has a repair guarantee. Compare the cost to comprehensive and collision insurance. Compare the increase to the cost of service contracts on household appliances ... which cost a much greater percentage of the purchase price. Compare the percentage increase in payment to the total payment: e.g. on a $300 payment, $10 a month is only 3% of the cost. Restate the cost in pennies per day or dollars per year. surely that is worth it, such complete protection for such a long time.

### "I want to think about it."

Use a waiver form. Explain that the law requires you to disclose all available warranties before the deal is done. A signature confirms that the customer was offered increased protection and declined. Another reason for taking the service contract now is that it can be included in the monthly payment. If the customer signs the waiver, explain that the service contract administrator will allow some time after the vehicle sale to add protection, but there are no price guarantees. Prices on extended service contracts rise on average about twice a year. Of course, if the vehicle is sold as a used car, the service contract is only available at the time of sale.

# Benefits of Service Contracts

> When one door closes, another opens.
> But, we often look so long and hard at the closed door, that we do not see the one that has opened for us.
>
> - Alexander G. Bell

- ❖ No limit on the number of claims that can be made.
- ❖ Policy available with no deductible
- ❖ Guarantees uninterrupted cross-country trip, providing rental cars.
- ❖ Increases resale value of vehicle, since it is transferable.
- ❖ Pays for out-of-state repairs with a credit card, avoiding reimbursement hassle.
- ❖ Hedges against inflation, using today's dollars for tomorrow's repairs.
- ❖ Pro-rated refund available. You only pay for what you use.
- ❖ Cost can be included in monthly payments or put on a credit card.
- ❖ Owner can use any licensed repair facility, including her own mechanic.
- ❖ Most repair claims are air-conditioning or electrical. Both are covered.
- ❖ Seals and Gaskets - all leaks - and all resulting damage is covered.
- ❖ Pays deductible on the factory warranty, covers rental car and towing.
- ❖ '800' line available in USA and Canada.
- ❖ Protects the owner against over-pricing or paying for unnecessary work.
- ❖ Many policies cover replacment of damaged tires
- ❖ The contract will always pay retail cost of parts and labor, whatever that cost will be 5 or 6 years from now.
- ❖ Most companies will allow new car coverage to be sold on vehicles that have some remaining factory warranty. The coverage is retro-active to the initial in-service date of the car. Start a follow-up program with the service department to contact those owners who are approaching the deadline

## Transfer Application

*[Form image: Transfer Application with fields for Year, Make, ID Number, Contract Number, Original Effective Date, Mileage, Transfer Date, Mileage, Original Contract Owner, Transfer To (New Owner), Street Address, City, State, Zip, Original Selling Dealer, Contract Holder Signature, Date, Authorized Dealer Signature, Date]*

**INSTRUCTIONS:**

1. This form must be received within 14 business days after sale of vehicle to the new owner.
2. Copies of all service records must accompany the transfer application.
3. A copy of the Bill of Sale must accompany the transfer application.
4. A copy of a federal Odometer Statement signed by both parties must accompany the application.

Have a supply of these forms to assist previous customers with transfers.

You may need different forms for each administrator.

There is usually a $25 fee.

## Cancellation Request

*[Form image: Cancellation Request with fields for Contract Number, Serial No., Dealer Code Number, Dealer Name, Contract Holder Name, Street Address, City/State/Zip, Effective Date, Contract Term-Yrs/Miles, Cancellation Date, Cancellation Mileage, Reason for Cancellation (Sale Unwound, Repossession, Vehicle Totalled, Customer Request, Other), Contract Holder Signature, Date, Requested By (Authorized Dealer Representative), Date]*

This is the form needed to obtain the pro-rated refund.

Administrators usually subtract a $25 or $50 fee and send the remaining premium to the dealership, with a letter indicating the refund factor.

The dealership applies the same refund factor to the retained profit, adds the dealership contribution to the total and cuts a check to the customer.

# Follow up Letter

Mr. John Customer
123 Main Street,
Anytown, CA 94530

Dear Mr. Customer:

I want to thank you personally for doing business with Everyday Motors.
Your satisfaction is our primary concern. If there is anything further that we can do in order to make your automobile experience first-class, please contact me directly.

In this regard, may I remind you of our extended service policy program. I believe that awareness of this program is more important than ever since our latest research indicates that our customers are keeping their cars longer. An average of four years is predicted for 1992. Our advice is that a seven year/100,000 mile extended service policy is virtually a win-win proposition.

- If you sell or trade the automobile in four years, you can transfer the remaining coverage. Offering a three-year service contract on a four-year old car will undoubtedly help you sell it. You will probably recover more than your original cost, since the price of service contracts rises every year, along with the price of everything else.

- If you keep the car for seven years, the odds do increase that you will need some work performed on the car. This certainly may not be the case, but if it is, inflation alone will double the cost of service. What will things cost in 1997? With this policy you are guaranteed that a covered repair will cost you nothing, not even a deductible.

If you have any further questions, please contact me at (408) 268-0136.

Sincerely,


Jan B. Strong

Customer Relations


**P.S.**

Bring this letter with you to the dealership, and Everyday Motors will contribute $100 to your purchase.

# Money Back Guarantee

> Don't let your mouth write no check that your tail can't cash.
>
> - Bo Diddley

Be very clear with the dealer principal on this technique. Make sure the conditions are acceptable.

The guarantee is a great incentive to 'buy today'.

The certificate answers the objection, "But I'll never use it."

"If you use it, it will pay for itself. If you transfer it, it will help you sell the car. If you never use it and you still have the car five (six or seven) years from now, we'll buy it back from you. you can't lose."

'Conditions' can include purchasing another vehicle from the dealership or getting the car serviced there.

The certificate should only be used as a closing tool. "If I did this for you, would you buy the service contract today?"

---

## MONEY BACK GUARANTEE
### EVERYDAY MOTORS

This certificate entitles the bearer to a refund of **100% of the purchase price** of the extended service contract described below, if it has not been used during the prescribed term.

Customer _____  Year, Make, Model _____
Address _____  Current Mileage _____
City, State, Zip _____  Service Contract Number _____
Contract Coverage _____  Contract Price _____
　　　　　　　　　　　　　　　　　　　　In Service Date _____

Conditions:
1. New vehicle extended service contract must be purchased from Everyday Motors.
2. Everyday Motors' sole obligation is the original selling price of the extended service contract. The policy must not have been used, abused, revoked, cancelled, transferred or devalued in any way.
3. 100% of the original price will be rebated or paid in cash upon the purchase of a new vehicle from Everyday Motors.
4. Refund only available to original purchaser, who must still own vehicle at time of expiration of coverage.

Customer Signature _____  Dealer Representative _____

# Notes

# Notes

# Credit Insurance

*Take time to deliberate,
but when the time for action
has arrived,
stop thinking and go in.*

*- Napoleon Bonaparte*

The priority of Life, Accident and Health insurance as an income producer in your department will vary according to the state in which you are working. Some states still allow 70% commission. Premium rate structures and commission schedules are set by each state ... and differ considerably. In California currently the commissions are set at 27.5% for Life and 23.75% for Accident and Health. Perhaps it is the low priority states that pull down the average, but statistics show that over 30% of the time customers are not even offered insurance at the point of the finance sale. The law requires disclosure of all available 'warranties' before the consummation of a sale. Asking for the sale is the first rule of selling.

The way to sell an 'intangible' product is to make it as 'tangible' as possible. Get to know your customer. Look at his age and occupation. Emphasize the benefits that suit the situation. To a 55 year-old customer, there is quite a benefit in being able to pay the same insurance premium as an 18 year-old. For many older people, credit insurance is by far the cheapest insurance available. Someone who works in a high risk occupation is obviously more likely to appreciate disability coverage. Finding the particular circumstances on which to place emphasis enables you to be enthusiastic about the real value of the product and the potential benefit to the customer.

Other good prospects might be customers with several dependents, or customers with considerable debt. Cosigners are more inclined to protect their credit against misfortune. With insurance sales, a personal example always helps to clarify the benefit. There is a true story of a 19 year-old woman in Southern Calfornia who financed her first new car and didn't even know there was credit insurance on the loan ... as sometimes used to happen. Unfortunately, she was involved in a very bad accident and her back was broken. She was in hospital for 6 months and then spent another 6 motnhs at home recuperating. When she returned to work, all her payments had been made on time. She was able to obtain her first major credit card, since her credit record was perfect.

The traditional approach to selling L,A&H insurance was the assumptive close. Occasionally the customer might not have been informed about the extra protection. More typically though, the insurance was disclosed during the readback of the contract. If the customer didn't object, the sale is closed. If the customer had an objection, that was the time to go into the presentation.

> If you would win a man
> to your cause,
> first convince him
> you are his sincere friend.
>
> - Abraham Lincoln

In the competitive buyer's market of the 1990's, customer shop not only price, but payment. Strong evidence of this is the proliferation of special factory finance programs and payment advertising. A customer who expects to see a certain payment, as a result of advertising or personal research, may resent being shown a payment that is higher because it includes insurance they did not request. They might become defensive and consequently not be open to your presentation. Respect the customer, indicate the features and benefits of the optional credit insurance and let them perceive the value relative to a small increase in payment.

Use the customer's own credit profile to show what happens when a loan goes delinquent. Fear of loss is a greater motivator than desire for gain. For most people, a credit rating is as important as their reputation. Benefits become tangible when related to the specific situation. It is *your* belief, *your* enthusiasm, that will convey as much meaning to the customer as any words you will use. Sell the program on its merits. Check with your carrier for the specifics about the coverage you have to offer.

> If there is any one secret of success, it lies in the ability to get the other person's point of view and see things from that person's angle as well as your own.
>
> - Henry Ford

You should introduce the subject of credit insurance as you discuss the financing terms and before any specifics have been quoted. Obviously factors like the amount financed and the downpayment will be affected by the addition of insurance. Introduce the subject as a good idea, given the particular profile of the customer in front of you. For example, when writing a cosigned loan:

"Often when we do co-signed business loans, the co-signer wants to know that the debt is secure. so I checked into this for you and it would only cost $15 a month.". Explain the benefits.

It may be more suitable to address the age of the customer:

"You know, Mr. Customer, there is a great benefit available to you in this state. For only $5 a month, you can get $20,000 worth of life insurance. I mention this because it really is a good deal. Normally, at your age, insurance would cost a lot more, as you're probably aware. We can do this since credit insurance inthis state is guaranteed issue ... no physical required. You are paying the same premium as an 18 year-old." Explain the benefits.

Always relate your presentation to your customer's circumstances:

"I don't usually emphasize disability insurance, Mr. Customer, but given your particular occupation - Nuclear Radiation Research - you might want to consider it. It is state-controlled and it is less expensive than regular insurance because it is designed to cover only this specific debt. No physical is required and all occupations are acceptable."

Disability insurance protects the customer's credit rating:

"You have perfect credit and you obviously make your paymetns on all these balances on time. Now might be a good time to add to your insurance coverage. Will your current insurance pay all these balances if you get sick and can't work? Disabability insurance, tied to this specific debt, is very affordable."

> There comes a time in the affairs of man when he must take the bull by the tail and face the situation.
>
> - W.C. Fields

The probability of a 30 year-old person becoming disabled for more than 3 months before age 65 is 1 in 2.

Approximately 70% of social security applicants do not qualify for full social security payments, under current qualification requirements.

From age 20 to 30, the chance that a person will suffer a prolonged disability (3 months or more) is virtually 3 times the chance that he or she will die.

Out of every 1000 workers age 20 to 30, as many as 789 will be disabled for at least 3 months before age 65.

Out of every 1000 workers age 35 to 40, as many as 685 will be disabled for at least 3 months before age 65 ... much greater odds.

In a study of U.S. mortgage foreclosures in the 1980's, it was found that 3% were caused by death and 48% by disability.

While approximately 150 million people in the USA have life insurance, only one third that many have private disability coverage.

By age 65:
At age 20, an American faces odds of 1:35 of dying and 1:10 of being disabled.
At age 30, ................................... of 1:29 of dying and 1:6 of being disabled.
At age 35, ................................... of 1:15 of dying and 1:5 of being disabled.
At age 40, ................................... of 1:10 of dying and 1:4 of being disabled.
At age 45, ................................... of 1:7 of dying and 1:3 of being disabled.
At age 50, ................................... of 1:4 of dying and 1:2 of being disabled.

The odds that a person will become disabled are greater than most of us would like to believe. The odds that a person will be prepared to handle the situation are even worse. We insure our deaths better than we do our lives.

## Objections

**"I don't need credit life insurance because I already have life insurance".**
Ask the customer how much his current policy provides. How much is her mortgage? Refer to any outstanding debt: "Do you have insurance on your mortgage loan? Most people change insurance infrequently and insurance coverage becomes out-dated. Taking inflation into account, less money ends up going to the surviving family than is usually anticipated.

**"I already have disability insurance"**
"What percentage of you income will it cover? What is the waiting period? What are the exclusions?" Workman's Compensation typically only covers about 60% of a person's income and only covers injuries in the workplace. *70% of disabilities are due to illness, which Worker's Compensation doesn't cover at all.* Other policies may cover up to 80% for qualified disabilities but may have term restrictions. Certainly the customer's original plan for coverage did not include this new financial commitment.

**"I have my own insurance agent."**
Hopefully, that agent is keeping the customer current with her insurance needs. However, credit insurance is really a different type of insurance. Rates are regulated by the state insurance commission and the coverage is designed only for the specific debt ... which has probably not been anticipated by the agent. for this reason, it is the cheapest insurance around and is only available when the customer signs the contract. It is also unlikely that the insurance the agent could provide would be guaranteed issue, thus requiring a physical, as well as age and sex adjustments. In other words, it would be more expensive.

**"I can buy insurance cheaper somewhere else."**
Probably not true. See above.

**"It makes the payments too high."**
Remind the customer that it is only so many pennies per day to protect a loss of (yearly salary) per year. After explaining the benefits of joint life and disability coverage, and the customer still objects to the increase in payment, move to the joint life coverage. The increase in payment should be a modest one. The bank automatically qualifies payment increases for insurance.

---

All things be ready,
if our minds be so.

- William Shakespeare

> No one likes to feel that he or she is being sold something or told to do a thing.
>
> We much prefer to feel that we are buying of our own accord or acting on our own ideas.
>
> We like to be consulted about our wishes, our wants, our thoughts.
>
> - Dale Carnegie

**"I'm young, single and healthy. Don't need it."**
you can't get insurance when you *need* it. Most young people have no insurance at all. If you get married or add other obligations to your life in the next 5 years, it will be more expensive then and you will appreciate this.

**"I have business insurance."**
"Surely that insurance is designed to protect your business while you can't work. Did the agent anticipate the addition of a car payment? To increase your business insurance is probably much more expensive than addinga couple of dollars a month.

**"I have equity in my houese for emergencies."**
Does the customer have insurance on the mortgage? 48% of mortgage foreclosures in this country are due to disability.

**"I have to think about it."**
Ask the customer his reason for waiting. Restate the objection. Explain the benefits. Emphasize that the benefits can only apply now, at contract signing. In the event of early payoff, unused premium is refunded. Have the customer initial the section of the contract waiving their right to life and disability coverage.

**Credit insurance is specific coverage for a certain amount of money that is extended on credit for a certain period of time. It is only active while the loan is in effect. The insurance terminates when the loan is paid off.**

**Finance Managers need a license to sell credit insurance.**

## Life Coverage:

**Joint Decreasing Life:** insurance on the lives of two joint and individually liable debtors, for a loan equal monthly installments over a specific period. The insurance coverage is reduced monthly by an amount equal to the loan payment. Benefits are paid upon the death of one of the debtors and insurance is consequently terminated on the survivor. If both die, only one claim is paid. The insurance includes unearned finance charges.

**Single Decreasing Life:** insurance on the primary debtor for a loan requiring equal monthly installmetns over a period of time. The insurance coverage is reduced monthly by an amount equal to the loan payment. The insurance includes unearned finance charges.

**Joint Net Decreasing Life:** insurance on the lives of two joint and individually liable debtors, for a loan equal monthly installments over a specific period. The insurance covers only the net principal balance (not the finance charges) of the loan and decreases as payments are made.

**Single Net Decreasing Life:** insurance covers only the net principal balance (not the finance charges) of the loan and decreases as payments are made.

**Level Life:** the amount of insurance remains constant over the term.

**Multi-Level Life:** level life coverages which decreases on a specific schedule, but not necessarily monthly.

## Disability Coverage (Accident and Health)

**14 Day Retroactive:** benefits are payable from the first day of absence from work, if the insured is sick for at least two weeks.

**30 Day Retroactive:** Covers from first day, after 30 days absence from work.

**14 Day Elimination:** Pays no benefits retroactively. Coverage begins on the 15th. day.

**30 Day Elimination:** Pays no benefits retroactively. coverage begins on 31st. day.

---

Whatever you vividly imagine,
ardently desire,
sincerely believe,
and enthusiastically act upon ...
must inevitably come to pass.

- Paul J. Meyer

---

Disability is defined as the inability to perform the duties of an occupation for which a person is reasonably suited by education, experience or training. Confirmation requires the signature of a doctor.

> The only way I can get you
> to do anything
> is by giving you what you want.
>
> - Dale Carnegie

- ❖ Present the most comprehensive coverage to the customers first. (Joint Life, Accident and Health)

- ❖ Offer a choice of Life, or Disability, or both.

- ❖ Relate a personal experience ... or that of someone you know.

- ❖ 'Guaranteed issue' insurance means no physical exam, no occupation restrictions and no age discrimination.

- ❖ The policy is non-cancellable, in case of changes in health or occupation.

- ❖ There is no waiting period. Coverage begins immediately.

- ❖ Standard rates: all ages pay the same premium.

- ❖ Typical coverage is for anything a doctor will sign. Hospitalization is not required.

- ❖ The policy pays regardless of what other coverage the customer may have.

- ❖ Coverage is available for cosigners.

- ❖ It is usually by far the cheapest insurance on the market, since it covers a specific debt and a specific payment.

- ❖ The premium can be included in the monthly payment.

- ❖ The retroactive coverage means that after the customer has been sick for a defined period of time, usually 14 days, the policy will pay for *all* the time lost.

- ❖ The cost of credit insurance is literally just pennies per day.

- ❖ Disability payments are made directly to the bank. There is no delay while the customer arranges paperwork. Installments are always paid on time.

- ❖ Refunds are pro-rated. You only pay for what you use.

- ❖ In the event of the death of the insured, the beneficiary receives title to the vehicle, free and clear ... as well as a check for the unearned finance charges.

- ❖ Whole Life or Term Insurance require a physical examination for substance abuse, cholesterol, obesity and smoking. Women pay higher premiums since they have a longer life expectancy and senior citizens pay higher premiums because they don't.

# Notes

# Notes

# Accessories

Serve and sell.

- Early IBM slogan

**The approach to selling accessories should be that you are providing a service.** While the vehicle is brand new is obviously the time to consider accessories, especially those involving appearance and protection. It is you, the finance manager, who offers these services because you are the one who can include them in the payment for the customer. This is true whether the payment will be on the finance contract, on a lease, on a special factory-subsidized program or through a credit union. If these products and services were purchased elsewhere, or at another time, the advantage of being able to include them in the payment would be lost. The opportunity to include the accessories as a simple addition to the month;y payment is a particular advantage if the financing is through one of the special low-rate, factory discount programs.

**The best way to present these services is to package them.** Packaging allows the customer to make choices ... not only between various groups, such as the Luxury Package or the Protection Package, but also within the group itself. This approach increases the odds that something the dealership has to offer can also be made to fit the customer's budget. For example, the customer may be attracted to a Sound System package but she may be reluctant to pay all the money necessary to upgrade the speakers, add an amplifier and a sub-woofer, and so on.... just adding a CD player might seem like a reasonable option.

**Experience will tell you which vehicles in your dealership are best suited for which optional packages.** Some cars will come from the factory with certain 'optional' accessories already intalled. Paint protection is more essential for certain colors and in certain parts of the country. 'Family' cars may need more interior prtoection. Always present everything and pay attention to what catches the customer's eye.

**As always, make the presentation before discussing cost.** It is building quite a hill to climb if you present each service separately, adding a cost step by step. Establish the value first. What the numbers will be depends on what choices the customer wants to make. Show the total cost of everything and go from there.

> The American system of ours, call it Americanism, call it Capitalism, call it what you like, gives each and every one of us a great opportuntiy,
> if we only seize it with both hands and make the most of it.
>
> - Al Capone

**Coordination with the sales department is essential.** Ideally, the finance manager has a clear agreement that all the accessories included in the deal before it reaches the finance office are costed out at full retail, with the gross attributed to F&I. This rarely happens. These situations still should be the exceptions to the rule. No finance manager can survive on a pay plan that includes selling custom wheels, for example, if the desk is consistently 'throwing in' the wheels 'at our cost' to make the deal. The sales manager should be getting paid on the F&I gross, so that she has an incentive to look for opportunities. If the buyer is locked in on price, for instance, there may be other avenues where money can be made. The two managers must work well together.

**Coordination with the service department is equally important**. Establish a fair cost to F&I for in-house accessories. For example, you should not have two hours retail labor to install paint protection. Accessories should be offered to customers at the same price throughout the store, so it is important that the cost to you be fair. Discuss this situation with the Dealer.

**There may be opportunities involving products and services not offered directly through the dealership**. Promote relationships with relaible sub-contractors for cellular telephones, alarms, radar detectors, CD systems and so on. Be sure that these vendors guarantee their work and have experience with your line of vehicles. they must be professional - on time consistently and available by telephone during the day. Unreliable sub-contractors will undermine your credibility and bring you nothing but problems. Reliable people will extend your range. They might even make presentations for you and install at the customer's home or office. They will provide promotional materials and assist with customer follow-up. They will also keep you up to date on the state of their particular art.

**Be creative in the way you package the accessories**. Be creative in the way you *sell* them. Appeal to the various emotions involved; the need for security; the fear of damage to a new car; the pride of showing the new car; the pleasure and sensation of the new sound system. Pay attention to the car. Look for a reaction. Often it becomes just a matter of price.

# Appearance Package

Sell when you can,
you are not for all markets.

- William Shalespeare

**NOVEMBER SPECIAL**
*Save money and protect your investment at the same time.*

PINSTRIPE

FLOOR MATS

PAINT PROTECTION

LEATHER PROTECTION

DOOR EDGE GUARDS

WHEEL WELL MOULDINGS

**SAVE $255**

**$745**

*Discover the pleasure of caring for your investment, let your pride in commitment, in long-term excellence, speak for itself.*

**An appearance package could be a desktop/shelf display, or it could be a laminated sheet that you present to the customer. A useful package might be:**

**Paint Protection:** a coating that guarantees to eliminate fading, oxidation and discoloration of paint for five years. No need to wax after application. If the vehicle is buffed out after several years, the buffing will not damage the paint.

**Fabric Protection:** seals the upholstery against most spills and stains. Offers protection against fading. Makes fabric softer and easier to clean.

**Leather Protection:** penetrates the pores of the leather and protects against fading, cracking and damage from spills and stains. Also protects vinyl tops.

**Sound insulation:** absorbs traffic and road noise. Adds an anti-corrosion agent designed to protect the vehicle against rust and dust, heat and cold.

**Pinstripe:** the crowning touch. Can be painted or taped. A hand-painted stripe is recommended. It should match the interior.

**Floor mats:** a necessity and a good item to include as a closer.

# Brochure

A custom brochure can be an effective way to present diverse aftermarket products

It can also be useful in follow-up mail.

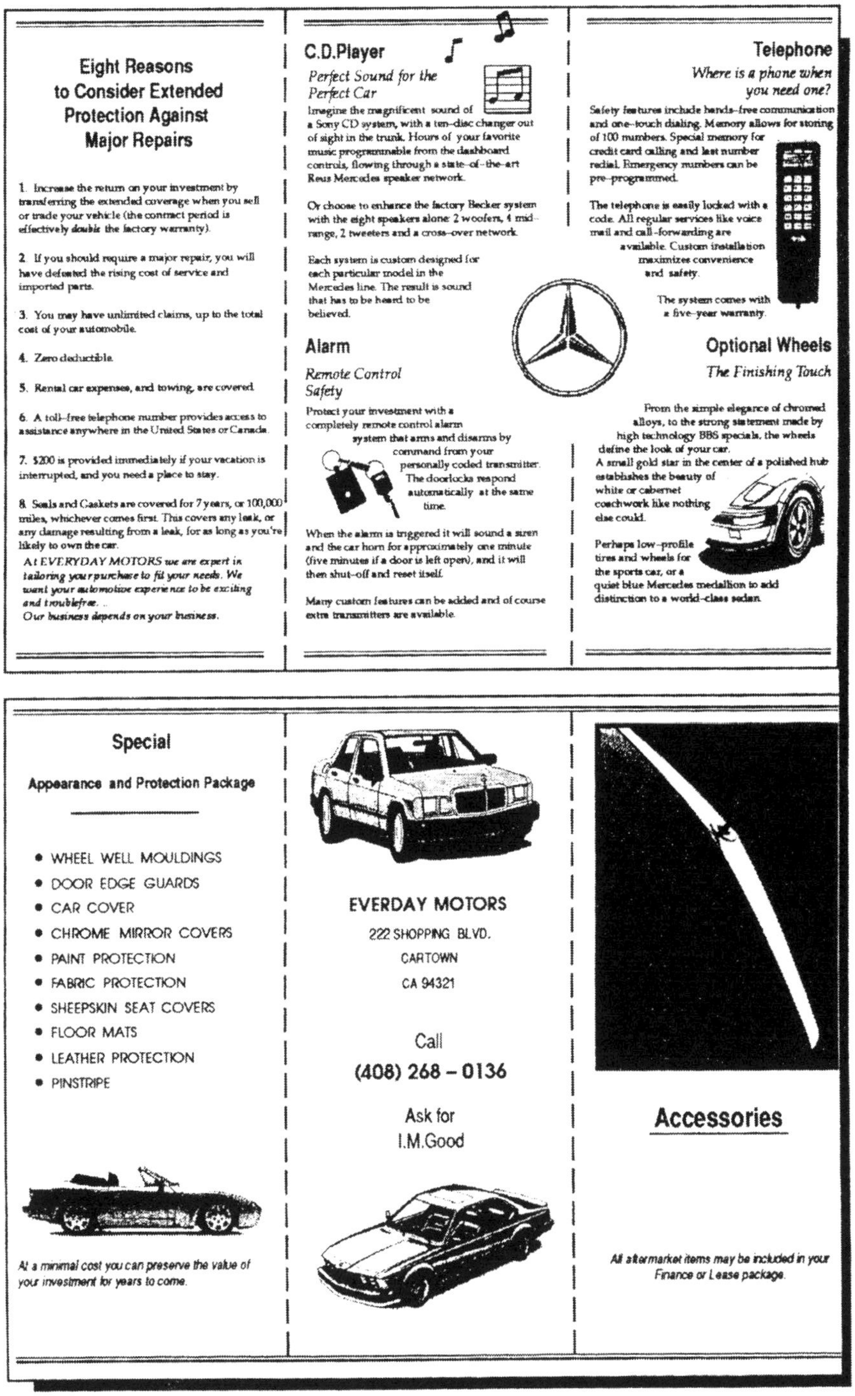

# Five Year Total Protection Package

| | |
|---|---|
| Extended Service Contract (7 year/100,000 miles) | $1495 |
| Appearance Package (Paint, Fabric, Underseal) | $995 |
| Security Package (Alarm, Remote Panic) | $795 |
| Total | $3285 |
| Total Package Discount (20%) | - $657 |
| **Keep your car safe, sound and looking like new for only** | $2638 |

- ❖ Pay attention to the customer. Which of the products is he most attracted to?

- ❖ There is a deadline on the opoortunity for a discount.

- ❖ Be prepared to combine elements from different packages or to single out one particular service.

- ❖ Emphasize the suitability of a particular package for a particular car ... appearance packages for family cars, luxury packages for coupes ....

- ❖ Make your presentations before discussing cost.

- ❖ Quote prices in terms of monthly payment when possible.

- ❖ Always quote the full package price first.

- ❖ Coordinate with sub-contractors (telephonoes, alarms, etc.) to offer a special package using their services and installed at the custoemr's home or work.

Accessories

# Products

So many products, so little time.

This is one reason why packaging is important.

| | |
|---|---|
| PINSTRIPE | CUSTOM WHEELS |
| PAINT PROTECTION | CUSTOM WOOD INTERIOR |
| FABRIC PROTECTION | CUSTOM STEERING WHEEL |
| LEATHER PROTECTION | SHIFT KNOB |
| SOUND INSULATION | CELLULAR PHONE |
| FLOOR MATS | CD PLAYER |
| CAR COVER | SPEAKER UPGRADE |
| DOOR EDGE GUARDS | STEREO UPGRADE |
| WHEEL WELL MOULDINGS | RADAR DETECTOR |
| SPOILER | WINDOW TINT |
| CHROME MIRROR COVERS | ALARM |

Assemble a **presentation book**, with pictures, showing:

- ❖ An older car, restored with paint protection
- ❖ Custom wheels
- ❖ Cellular telephones
- ❖ Alarms

and so on....

Be prepared to SHOW the customer what yu have to offer.

**Feature a different package as a special in each issue of the newsletter.**

# Notes

# Notes

# Appendices

# Appendix A: DMV Forms

## Demonstrators and Executive Cars

This form is to be used for vehicles which have been operated by a dealer, distributor or manufacturer. They have been driven on special plates and consequently have not been previously registered. The customer is showing that he knows the car he is buying was used as a demonstrator.

The vehicle is transferred on a new car Report of Sale.

This form cannot be signed by use of power of attorney.

Only one registered owner needs to sign.

If a vehicle has been previously registered, regardless of to whom, this form does not apply and the vehicle is transferred on a Used Car Report of Sale.

## Non-resident Military

The vehicle is transferred on a new car Report of Sale as usual.

The customer must be stationed in this state and list an out-of-state residence.

The exemption is from license fees, not registration, transfer or weight fees.

This form cannot be signed using power of attorney.

If the customer ordered personalized plates, the usual fees apply.

# Statement of Facts Environmental Plates

The customer may attach the plates to another car (box 3) or keep the plates for later (box 5).

Note the renewal fee if the customer keeps the plates.

Power of attorney may not be used.

# Plate Interchange

This form is used to transfer personalized, disability, ham operator or veteran plates to another vehicle. If these plates are being assigned a vehicle that already has plates, the old plates are surrendered to the DMV.

If there is time remaining on the tags for the plates, pro-rated credit is given for that time and new tags are issued. Collect the full transfer fee ($40 in California) and refund the difference once fees are confirmed.

It is recommended only to handle a transfer if the 'source' vehicle is being traded in. Otherwise, taking the plates of of a different car, the customer may be making that vehicle illegal on the street. The customer can obtain a temporary registration from the DMV for the 'source' vehicle.

Be sure and note the characters on the plate.

A power of attorney may not be used..

## Environmental License Plates

Encourage two choices: no less than three characters, no more than seven.

Offer a piece of paper on which to practice first.

Explain that if both choices are taken, the customer will be issued regular plates and refunded the difference in fees. They can then, if they are brave, venture into the DMV and ask those inside to explore the computer for choices that have not been taken.

Dashes ... stars ... pictures ...etc. are not permitted.

In California, the fee is $36 for reflectorized plates, $35 for blue and gold.

Be sure the printing is clear and legible.

It is mandatory to complete the statement explaining the 'meaning' of the choice.

In California, these license plates are called 'environmental', since the fees are supposed to provide extra funding to protect the environment.

An extra $20 is inthe yearly renewal fee.

## Statement of Error or Erasure

This form is required when an error has been made on either side of an ownership certificate.

Only the person who made the error may sign the form.

If the registered owner incorrectly signed the title, then she would have to sign the statement of error.

Power of attorney may not be used.

## Bill of Sale

This form is most commonly used when a vehicle is traded in by a customer who is not shown as the registered owner. In this case, there must be a bill of sale from the registered owner to the trade customer.

Technically, when a 'rollback' occurs, the customer who is 'rolled back' should sign a bill of sale back to the dealer.

Often a power of attorney is used for this.

## Lien Satisfied

This form is most commonly used when a non-resident vehicle is being registered in California and the out-of-state title has not been properly signed off by the legal owner.

Any time a title or duplicate title still shows a lienholder, and the title has not been counter-signed by the lienholder, this form should be signed by the institution involved.

The form must be signed by an authorized agent of the insitution cited on the title.

Power of attorney may not be used.

## Name Statement

This form is used when there are discrepancies in the way the names on a document are mis-stated or mis-spelled. Those situations may be:

A married person whose registration shows a maiden name.

A person who signs a document not showing a personal title, although the registration shows one ... such as Jr., Sr., etc.

A simple mis-spelling or typographical error

Power of attorney may not be used.

## Statement of Facts

This form is rmost commonly used when no other form will do. It is used for solving any transfer problem which is out of the ordinary.

The form may be used by an owner to state legally that the vehicle has never been involved in an accident.

A statement that the vehicle is free from all liens and encumbrances, when a title is not immediately available.

This form may be used to confirm any promises or conditions that have become part of the vehicle transfer.

In most cases, this form will not be sent to the DMV but kept on file.

Power of attorney may not be used.

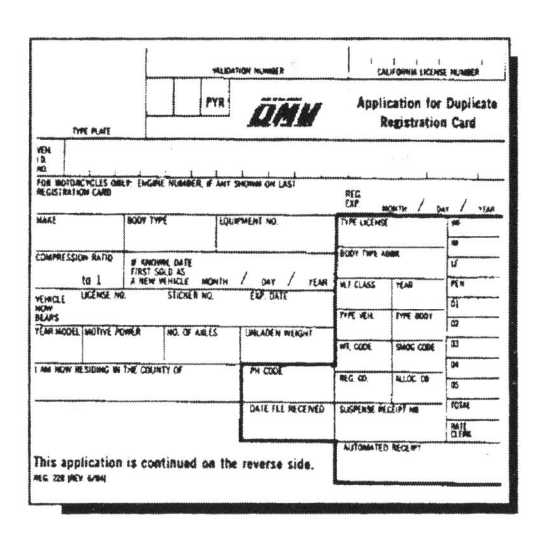

## Application for Duplicate Registration

This form is used when a registration has been lost or destroyed.

A $7 fee is required

This form is not required for transfer of the vehicle, since a DMV printout may be used.

Look for license fees and penalties due, since the registration may have expired.

Be sure to obtain the vehicle ID number.

A power of attorney may not be used.

## Application for Duplicate Title (Front)

This form is used whenever the ownership certificate is lost or destroyed ... or never received. It cannot be used while a title is inthe process of being issued.

The DMV created this new form to include 'paperless' transactions

For questions on 'paperless' transactions, send a non-letter to the state capital.

Or call the DMV and describe what you have in front of you.

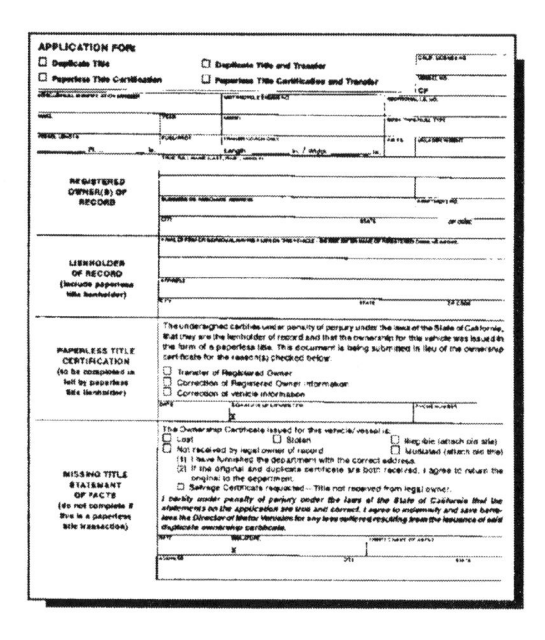

## Application for Duplicate Title (Back)

The back of this form requires carefull attention to the signatures.

A $7 fee is required.

If there are two registered owners, make sure they both sign the first section.

The legal owner, even if it is the same person (people), must sign the second section, or a Statement of Lien Satisfied may be attached.

Usually the dealership (DMV secretary) will sign the third section. The dealer will sign the bottom of the form if it is a request for a title that was never received.

Power of attorney may be used.

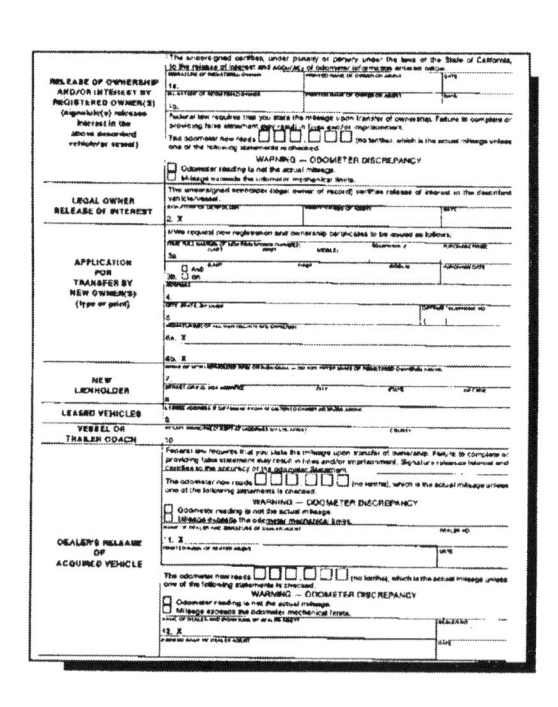

# Appendix A: DMV Forms

## Commercial Registration

This form is rmost commonly used for trucks used for business. Also applies to taxicabs and limousines.

Be sure the appropriate box is checked.

If the vehicle is over 6000 pounds, a weight certificate must be included.

In the case of joint registration, only one person needs to sign.

Power of attorney may not be used.

## Title Only Transfer

This form is required whenever a vehicle is purchased but is not going to be operated on the state highways.

The customer need not pay license or regstration fees.

A separate $35 fee is required.

'Title Only' applies to new cars, 'Transfer Only' applies to used cars.

The vehicle must be delivered on dealer plates, by use of a trip permit or directly to the shipping agent.

A Report of Sale must be submitted to the DMV.

A power of attorney may be used.

149

# Appendix B: Laws and Taxes

## Sales Tax

### Taxable Sales

- Reports of Sale books and other records relative to sales tax must be maintained for four years.
- All dealer-installed accessories, such as luggage racks, custom wheels, sound systems, paint treatments and undercoating are part of the taxable sales price of a vehicle.
- Charges for the document preparation are subject to tax.
- Charges for smog certificate inspections are subject to tax. The charge for the certificate itself is exempt.
- Reconditioning costs paid by the dealer as a condition of the sale are subject to tax.
- Underallowances on trade-iins are subject to tax.
- Mandatory warranty charges, if separately stated, are subject to tax.
- Vehicles sold to members of the armed services are subject to tax.
- Vehicles picked up by out-of-state residents are subject to tax.

### Non-taxable Sales

- Vehicle license fees, including trasnfer fees, are exempt. Excess license fees collected and not returned are subject to tax
- Separately-stated finance and interest charges are not taxable.
- Separately-stated insurance charges are not taxable.
- Optional warranties are exempt.
- Vehicles used only for demonstration and display are not taxable.
- Vehicles shipped or delivered out-of-state and used out-of-state for more than 90 days are not taxable.
- Vehicles sold for resale to an agent with a resale license are not taxable.
- Vehicles sold and registered to a leasing company are not taxable.

## Luxury Tax Exemption

This form is should now accompany the resale card in any transaction where taxes are waived.

## Out-of-State Delivery

This form should be signed by every customer who takes delivery of a vehicle out-of-state.

The vehicle must be delivered by a representative of the selling dealership or a professional delivery company.

Shipping must be arranged by the dealership, not by the customer.

## Resale Card

Any sale 'for resale' to a new car dealer requires only that a 'general' card, with the other dealer's resale number be on file.

A sale 'for resale' to any other party requires that a specific card be on file for each transaction, including the ID number of the vehicle specified.

If the dealer registers the car on behalf of a leasing company, license fees must be paid.

If you are not familiar with the buyer, you should request a copy of the resale license.

## Tax Declaration

This form should be signed by every customer whose residence is outside the county in which the dealership is located.

This form would document the reason for collecting tax at any rate other than the local county. For example, in Northern California, some counties do not collect mass transit tax.

The customer is taxed at the rate pertaining to their county of residence.

# California Sales Tax Chart by County

| County | July 15, 1991 | Revised | County | July 15, 1991 | Revised |
|---|---|---|---|---|---|
| Alameda | 8.25% | | Orange | 7.75% | |
| Alpine | 7.25% | | Placer | 7.25% | |
| Amador | 7.25% | | Plumas | 7.25% | |
| Butte | 7.25% | | Riverside | 7.75% | |
| Calaveras | 7.25% | | Sacramento | 7.75% | |
| Colusa | 7.25% | | San Benito | 7.75% | |
| Contra Costa | 8.25% | | San Bernadino | 7.75% | |
| Del Norte | 7.25% | | San Diego | 8.25% | |
| El Dorado | 7.25% | | San Francisco | 8.25% | |
| Fresno | 7.75% | | San Joaquin | 7.75% | |
| Glenn | 7.25% | | San Luis Obispo | 7.25% | |
| Humboldt | 7.25% | | San Mateo | 8.25% | |
| Imperial | 7.75% | | Santa Barbara | 7.75% | |
| Inyo | 7.75% | | Santa Clara | 8.25% | |
| Kern | 7.25% | | Santa Cruz | 8.25% | |
| Kings | 7.25% | | Shasta | 7.25% | |
| Lake | 7.25% | | Sierra | 7.25% | |
| Lassen | 7.25% | | Siskiyou | 7.25% | |
| Los Angeles | 8.25% | | Solano | 7.25% | |
| Madera | 7.75% | | Sonoma | 7.50% | |
| Marin | 7.25% | | Stanislaus | 7.25% | |
| Mariposa | 7.25% | | Sutter | 7.25% | |
| Mendocino | 7.25% | | Tehama | 7.25% | |
| Merced | 7.25% | | Trinity | 7.25% | |
| Modoc | 7.25% | | Tulare | 7.25% | |
| Mono | 7.25% | | Tuolumne | 7.25% | |
| Monterey | 7.75% | | Ventura | 7.25% | |
| Napa | 7.25% | | Yolo | 7.25% | |
| Nevada | 7.25% | | Yuba | 7.25% | |

# Luxury Tax

- ❖ The Luxury tax is on sales of automobiles above $30,000 which have an unloaded weight of 6,000 pounds or less, and on limousines, regardless of weight. Multi-purpose vehicles are considered "trucks" in these regulations.

- ❖ The tax is paid on the retail price including the gas guzzler tax, parts and accessories, any goods and services the customer is required to buy, and any costs incurred while getting the vehicle ready for sale, including transportation and insurance.

- ❖ Optional extended warranties, state title, registration and license fees are not included in the price.

- ❖ Exempt vehicles are those for use as police, fire-fighting, search and rescue, public safety, public works, taxicabs or emergency vehicles.

- ❖ Parts and accessories for a luxury vehicle that exceed a total price of $200 and are added within six months of original purchase are also to be taxed.

- ❖ No tax is owed on any imported vehicle that was used outside the United States before January 1, 1991.

- ❖ The tax does not apply to used cars sold before January 1, 1991.

- ❖ Demonstrators used after January 1, 1991 are subject to the tax based on fair market value. No dealer is liable for use tax on a passenger vehicle that has been driven less than 200 miles.

- ❖ On a retail purchase, the buyer is responsible for the tax. On a lease, the lessor is responsible.

- ❖ A refund is permitted if the first retail sale is rescinded at any time.

# Regulation Z: Truth in Lending Act

- The purpose of the law is to make clear to consumers the cost of credit.

- It is the Truth-in-Lending Act that requires the disclosure boxes that summarize a finance contract. Required disclosures are: Annual Percentage Rate, Finance Charge, Total of Payments and Total Sale Price.

- The law also requires that these disclosures be paid in any credit advertising.

- All other charges relating to the transaction must also be disclosed: taxes, official fees and insurance.

- The customer must acknowledge the disclosure. Usually a statement on the document, located near the customer signature line, indicates receipt of a copy.

- The total cost of credit may be disclosed in a document separate from the contract, as long as this occurs before the final transaction is signed.

- If there is more than one borrower involved in the transaction, still only one copy of the documents need be provided.

- Adjustments to the contract after disclosure do not violate the law. However, the customer has no obligation to sign a new contract.

- If a mistake, or inaccurate disclosure, is made, the creditor has 15 days to notify the customer and rectify the situation. The lender must ensure that the borrower will not pay a finance charge in excess of the amount dictated by the Annual Percentage Rate actually disclosed.

- The amount of, or method for determining, any penalty for delinquency, default or pre-payment must be disclosed.

# Consumer Leasing Act

- ❖ This act requires significant disclosure to the consumer.

- ❖ The property to be leased must be identified specifically.

- ❖ Initial fees paid at lease signing, must be itemized.

- ❖ The payment schedule, total of payments, and official fees (license and taxes) must be disclosed.

- ❖ Additional fees, including (on an open-end lease) the potential difference between the residual value and the market value, must be disclosed.

- ❖ There must be a statement clarifying any express warranties or guarantees made by the lessor or the manufacturer.

- ❖ Identification of the party responsible for maintaining the vehicle, as well as standards for reasonable wear and tear, must be clear.

- ❖ Any security interest retained by the lessor must be described.

- ❖ The amount, or method for determining the amount, of penalty for delinquency or default must be disclosed.

- ❖ There must be a statement of whether or not the lessee has the right to purchase the property. If so, then how, when and for how much.

- ❖ There must be a statement of conditions under which the lease may be terminated prior to term and the penalties involved, if any.

- ❖ On an open-end lease, there must be a statement that if, at termination, the market value of the vehicle is significantly lower than the anticipated (residual) value, the lessee's liablility shall be limited to the sum of three monthly payments, unless the lessor is willing to go to court and pay the lessee's legal fees.

- ❖ The value of the property at the beginning of the lease, the specific and total lease obligation at termination, and the difference between them, must be itemized.

# The Equal Opportunity Credit Act

- ❖ Discrimination is prohibited on the basis of sex, marital status, race, color, religion, national origin, age, acceptance of public assistance or the exercise of consumer rights.

- ❖ Creditors (lenders) must inform the credit reporting agency if the account they are listing is in the name of both spouses. The bureau must list the account accordingly ... in both names.

- ❖ Creditors must notify applicants within a reasonable time of the action taken on their application. Those denied credit must be informed of the reasons for the denial.

- ❖ Creditors must keep all the applications, and all relevant material, for a minimum of 25 months after supplying the consumer with a notice of action.

- ❖ Creditors may not close an account, or change the status of an account, solely due to a change in marital status (or in sex). Exception can be made if the original approval required the income of both spouses.

- ❖ Creditors must respond to written requests for an explanation of credit status.

- ❖ Separate accounts may not be denied to an applicant on the basis of sex or marital status. Information on sex and marital status may not be requested.

- ❖ Lenders may not request information about birth control practices or child-bearing plans or potential.

- ❖ The information about the income of a spouse must be considered in the qualifying process, if provided.

- ❖ Credit scoring programs may not use sex or marital status information.

- ❖ Lenders may not make discouraging statements to applicants regarding sex or marital status.

- ❖ Information regarding alimony, child support or maintenance payments may not be sought by a creditor without the applicant's consent.

# The Magnuson-Moss Warranty Act

The Magnuson-Moss Warranty Act, along with the Uniform Commercial Code, sets forth the rules on warranty disclosures and how to settle warranty claims. It covers both express and implied warranties:

## Expressed warranty

- Any statement or act on the part of the seller to the buyer automatically becomes part of the contract.
- The warranty can be verbal. It does not have to be written.
- No specific intent to convey a warranty is required.
- This statement - the expressed warranty - can occur before or after the consummation of a contract.

## Implied Warranty

- A reasonable expectation on the part of the buyer that the product will perform as advertised or promised.
- An implied warranty is in effect even if the customer has other warranties in writing.
- If a customer asks to see a service contract that 'covers everything on the car' and the finance manager suggests a particular service contract in response, it may be considered an implied warranty unless what is not covered is disclosed.

This legislation is intended to give a consumer legal recourse if a product (car, service contract, alarm system, paint protection, etc.) does not perform as promised, either expressly or by implication. The point is that the warranty does not have to be in writing. You are accountable for what you say. If an implied warranty was not intended, the burden is on the seller to provide clear and convincing evidence.

# Appendix C: A.P.R. to Add-on Rates

(based on $10,000 Amount Financed)

|  | | \multicolumn{10}{c}{Term in months} |
|---|---|---|---|---|---|---|---|---|---|---|---|
|  | | 6 | 12 | 18 | 24 | 30 | 36 | 42 | 48 | 54 | 60 |
| A | 8.00% | 4.69 | 4.39 | 4.30 | 4.27 | 4.27 | 4.27 | 4.28 | 4.30 | 4.31 | 4.33 |
|   | 8.25% | 4.84 | 4.52 | 4.44 | 4.41 | 4.40 | 4.41 | 4.42 | 4.44 | 4.46 | 4.48 |
| P | 8.50% | 4.99 | 4.66 | 4.58 | 4.55 | 4.54 | 4.55 | 4.56 | 4.58 | 4.60 | 4.62 |
|   | 8.75% | 5.14 | 4.80 | 4.71 | 4.68 | 4.68 | 4.69 | 4.70 | 4.72 | 4.74 | 4.76 |
| R |  |  |  |  |  |  |  |  |  |  |  |
|   | 9.00% | 5.28 | 4.94 | 4.85 | 4.82 | 4.82 | 4.83 | 4.84 | 4.86 | 4.89 | 4.91 |
|   | 9.25% | 5.43 | 5.08 | 4.99 | 4.96 | 4.96 | 4.97 | 4.98 | 5.00 | 5.03 | 5.06 |
|   | 9.50% | 5.58 | 5.22 | 5.13 | 5.10 | 5.10 | 5.11 | 5.12 | 5.15 | 5.17 | 5.20 |
|   | 9.75% | 5.73 | 5.36 | 5.26 | 5.24 | 5.23 | 5.25 | 5.27 | 5.29 | 5.32 | 5.35 |
|   | 10.00% | 5.87 | 5.50 | 5.40 | 5.37 | 5.37 | 5.39 | 5.41 | 5.44 | 5.46 | 5.50 |
|   | 10.50% | 6.17 | 5.78 | 5.68 | 5.65 | 5.67 | 5.65 | 5.69 | 5.72 | 5.76 | 5.79 |
|   | 11.00% | 6.47 | 6.06 | 5.96 | 5.93 | 5.93 | 5.95 | 5.98 | 6.01 | 6.05 | 6.09 |
|   | 11.50% | 6.76 | 6.34 | 6.23 | 6.21 | 6.22 | 6.24 | 6.27 | 6.31 | 6.35 | 6.39 |
|   | 12.00% | 7.06 | 6.62 | 6.51 | 6.49 | 6.50 | 6.52 | 6.56 | 6.60 | 6.65 | 6.69 |
|   | 12.50% | 7.35 | 6.90 | 6.79 | 6.77 | 6.78 | 6.81 | 6.85 | 6.90 | 6.95 | 7.00 |
|   | 13.00% | 7.65 | 7.18 | 7.07 | 7.05 | 7.07 | 7.10 | 7.14 | 7.19 | 7.25 | 7.30 |
|   | 13.50% | 7.95 | 7.46 | 7.35 | 7.33 | 7.35 | 7.39 | 7.44 | 7.49 | 7.55 | 7.61 |
|   | 14.00% | 8.25 | 7.74 | 7.63 | 7.62 | 7.64 | 7.68 | 7.73 | 7.79 | 7.86 | 7.92 |
|   | 14.50% | 8.54 | 8.03 | 7.91 | 7.90 | 7.93 | 7.97 | 8.03 | 8.09 | 8.16 | 8.23 |
|   | 15.00% | 8.84 | 8.31 | 8.20 | 8.18 | 8.21 | 8.27 | 8.33 | 8.40 | 8.47 | 8.55 |
|   | 15.50% | 9.14 | 8.59 | 8.48 | 8.47 | 8.50 | 8.56 | 8.63 | 8.70 | 8.78 | 8.86 |
|   | 16.00% | 9.44 | 8.88 | 8.76 | 8.76 | 8.79 | 8.86 | 8.93 | 9.01 | 9.09 | 9.18 |
|   | 16.50% | 9.73 | 9.16 | 9.04 | 9.04 | 9.09 | 9.15 | 9.23 | 9.32 | 9.41 | 9.50 |
|   | 17.00% | 10.03 | 9.45 | 9.33 | 9.33 | 9.38 | 9.45 | 9.53 | 9.63 | 9.72 | 9.82 |
|   | 17.50% | 10.33 | 9.73 | 9.61 | 9.62 | 9.67 | 9.75 | 9.84 | 9.94 | 10.04 | 10.15 |
|   | 18.00% | 10.63 | 10.02 | 9.90 | 9.91 | 9.97 | 10.05 | 10.15 | 10.25 | 10.36 | 10.47 |
|   | 18.50% | 10.93 | 10.30 | 10.19 | 10.20 | 10.26 | 10.35 | 10.45 | 10.56 | 10.68 | 10.80 |
|   | 19.00% | 11.23 | 10.59 | 10.47 | 10.49 | 10.56 | 10.65 | 10.76 | 10.88 | 11.00 | 11.13 |
|   | 19.50% | 11.53 | 10.87 | 10.76 | 10.78 | 10.86 | 10.96 | 11.07 | 11.20 | 11.33 | 11.46 |
|   | 20.00% | 11.83 | 11.16 | 11.05 | 11.07 | 11.16 | 11.26 | 11.39 | 11.52 | 11.65 | 11.79 |
|   | 20.50% | 12.13 | 11.45 | 11.34 | 11.37 | 11.46 | 11.57 | 11.70 | 11.84 | 11.98 | 12.13 |
|   | 21.00% | 12.43 | 11.74 | 11.63 | 11.66 | 11.76 | 11.88 | 12.01 | 12.16 | 12.31 | 12.46 |
|   | 21.50% | 12.73 | 12.02 | 11.92 | 11.96 | 12.06 | 12.19 | 12.33 | 12.48 | 12.64 | 12.80 |

The Complete F&I Reference Book

# Appendix D: Schedule C
## Income Verification for self-employed individual

Note that even though the business lost money (-$500 bottom line), Car and truck expenses ($3000) and Depreciation ($2500) add $5500 to the customer's income.

Gross income to business before expenses........................

Car and Truck expenses...........

Depreciation ............................

❖ Gross Income to the business is not gross income to the individual.

❖ Car and Truck expenses can be added back to income.

❖ Depreciation can be added back to income.

❖ If the customer also owns rental property, be sure to obtain the Schedule E of the tax return, in order to add back the real estate depreciation.

# Appendix E: Deal Forms

## Rescission Agreement

This form should be included in every deal where the vehicle is not paid for in full.

Check the box for the kind of income verification the customer has agreed to provide.

Enter the figure for the amount of income the customer claims to be able to prove.

---

**ATTACHMENT " A "**
**RESCISSION AGREEMENT**

This attachment is part of the attached agreement so that this page and the attached agreement, taken together, are a single document and a single contract.

Buyer acknowledges that it is the intent of Buyer and Seller that this contract be sold and assigned to a financial institution. To facilitate the assignment, Buyer agrees to furnish credit-related documentation as requested by Seller as follows:

❑ Current Tax Return for 19____
  Showing $_____
  reported as adjusted gross income

❑ Current Tax Returns for the years
  19____ to 19____

❑ Current Pay Stub indicating an
  average monthly income of
  $_____ for the last three months

❑ Notice of Co-Signer (Co-Purchaser)

❑ Guarantee

❑ Current Registration on
  Trade-in vehicle

❑ Personal Financial Statement

❑ Corporate Tax return

❑ Current W-2 19____ to 19____

❑ Business Credit Application

❑ Insurance Binder

❑ Corporate Resolution with Corporate Seal

❑ Business Financial Statement
  19____ to 19____

❑ Title on Trade-in vehicle

❑ Other _____

Buyer agrees to furnish Buyer's insurance company with information needed to obtain insurance within three days, and Buyer will furnish Seller's Finance Department with a correct telephone number and a contact person at Buyer's insurance agency as soon as possible.

If, for any reason, Seller is unable to assign this contract to any one of the financial institutions with whom it does business pursuant to assignment terms acceptable to the Seller, BUYER UPON NOTICE SHALL IMMEDIATELY RETURN TO SELLER ALL CONSIDERATIONS RECEIVED UNDER THE CONTRACT, INCLUDING THE VEHICLE. Such notice shall be given by first-class mail addressed to Buyer at the address shown for Buyer in this contract or by any method giving actual notice to Buyer.

Upon Buyer's return of the vehicle and any other consideration pursuant to this attachment, Seller shall immediately return to Buyer all consideration received under this contract, including the downpayment and the trade-in vehicle, if any. Upon exchange of all consideration, the contract shall be deemed rescinded.

If the vehicle has been damaged while in Buyer's possession or control before it is returned to Seller under the terms of this attachment, Buyer shall pay Seller the reasonable retail cost of repair.

As a condition of the purchase of this vehicle, Buyer agrees to furnish the above items. Buyer understands that Seller needs these items as quickly as possible to obtain vehicle registration and/or auto financing. Buyer also understands that if Buyer can not supply Seller with the above within ten days from the date of purchase, Buyer may be subject to a late charge of as much as 5% of the outstanding balance.

If and when a financial institution agrees to purchase this contract on terms acceptable to the Seller, the provisions of this attachment will immediately be cancelled, this attachment will no longer be part of the contract, and Seller will detach this page from the remainder of the contract prior to physical delivery of the contract to the financial institution. If the financial institution thereafter fails for any reason to complete the purchase of the contract, this attachment will be revived, and the Seller will re-attach it to the contract.

By initialling below, Buyer acknowledges having read and received a legible copy of this attachment.

_____    _____
Buyer's initials               Co-Buyer's initials

# Recap Sheet

A recap sheet will summarize for the finance manager all the elements of the deal.

When this sheet is on the cover of the deal jacket, another manager is able to determine the status of a deal while it is pending approval with a lender.

| COVER SHEET | | |
|---|---|---|
| CUSTOMER _____ SALESPERSON #1 _____ SALESPERSON #2 _____ | | |
| DATE ____ STOCK # ____ MAKE ____ MODEL ____ MANAGER ____ | | |

| SALES RECAP | TRADE | CHECK-LIST |
|---|---|---|
| SELLING PRICE ____ | 1. YEAR ____ MAKE ____ | COPY OF DRIVER'S LICENSE ☐ |
| ADDITIONS ____ | WHOLESALE BOOK ____ | STOCK CARD ☐ |
| ____ | ACV ____ | SIGNED CREDIT APP. ☐ |
| ____ | PAYOFF ____ | VIN # FROM CAR ☐ |
| ____ | GOOD UNTIL ____ | |
| TRADE ALLOWANCE 1. ____ | BANK ____ | U/C WINDOW STICKER ☐ |
| 2. ____ | PHONE # ____ | U/C LICENSE FEES ☐ |
| | VERIFIED BY ____ | EXPIRATION DATE ☐ |
| CASH DOWN ____ | ACCOUNT # ____ | EXACT MILES ☐ |
| | REG. ____ PINK ____ | ACV SHEET ☐ |
| FINANCE RATE ____ | | TRADE MILES ☐ |
| TERMS ____ | | |
| | 2. YEAR ____ MAKE ____ | **INSURANCE** |
| M.S.R.P. ____ | WHOLESALE BOOK ____ | |
| LEASE FACTOR ____ | ACV ____ | COMPANY ____ |
| CAP REDUCTION ____ | PAYOFF ____ | AGENT ____ |
| TERMS ____ | GOOD UNTIL ____ | PHONE # ____ |
| RESIDUAL ____ | BANK ____ | POLICY # ____ |
| BANK ____ | PHONE # ____ | |
| | VERIFIED BY ____ | |
| MANAGER APPROVAL ____ | ACCOUNT # ____ | |
| | REG. ____ PINK ____ | |

| FINANCE INFORMATION | | | |
|---|---|---|---|
| BANK | BANK | BANK | BANK |
| DATE | DATE | DATE | DATE |
| RESPONSE | RESPONSE | RESPONSE | RESPONSE |
| NAME | NAME | NAME | NAME |
| STIPULATIONS | STIPULATIONS | STIPULATIONS | STIPULATIONS |

# Follow Up

Sometmes you may need to emphasize a certain point.

The One Pay contract is due, and there will be a late penalty.

**IMPORTANT**

As a condition of the purchase of an automobile from Everyday Motors, I promise to pay the outstanding balance by _____.

I agree that if I have not presented the funds required by this date, Everyday Motors should place the contract I have signed with a bank of their choosing, and that I will provide all the documentation necessary to implement that process.

I understand that if Everyday Motors does not receive the balance within 10 days from the date of purchase, I am subject to a 5% late charge.

_____        _____
Signature                                              Date

Insurance verification is one of the major obstacles to timely funding of contracts and leases. Give one of these cards to every customer.

Reminds the customer to add the vehicle to his policy and notify the lienholder.

**Everyday Motors**
222 Shopping Boulevard • Cartown California
94321

To: Insurance Agent
From: Everyday Motors

Please be advised that the lienholder for our customer's car will be:

Motor Car Acceptance Corporation
P.O. Box 5000
Roseland, Texas
77887

Your assistance in verifying insurance would be greatly appreciated. Please call MCAC at 800 777-4456 and ask for Mable.
If you have any questions, call Jan Strong at Everyday Motors • (408) 233-3344.
Thank You.

An ounce of prevention is easily worth a pound of cure.
Give the customer a tangible reminder of steps to be completed.

## Weekly Log

### WEEKLY RECAP

Date: From:          To:

|  | New Car | New Truck | Used | Other | Total |
|---|---|---|---|---|---|
| **Total Sales** | | | | | |
| **Fleet & Lease** | | | | | |
| **Retail Units Verified** | | | | | |
| **Finance Penetration** / Reserve | # / % / $ | # / % / $ | # / % / $ | # / % / $ | # / % / $ |
| **LAHA Penetration** / Income | # / % / $ | # / % / $ | # / % / $ | # / % / $ | # / % / $ |
| **VSC Penetration** / Income | # / % / $ | # / % / $ | # / % / $ | # / % / $ | # / % / $ |
| **Anti-Theft Penetration** / Income | # / % / $ | # / % / $ | # / % / $ | # / % / $ | # / % / $ |
| **Appearance Pkg. Penetration** / Income | # / % / $ | # / % / $ | # / % / $ | # / % / $ | # / % / $ |
| **Department Income** | | | | | |
| **$ Per Finance Deal** | | | | | |
| **$ Per Retail Unit** | | | | | |
| **Objective $ Per Retail Unit** | | | | | |

## Call Log

| | | LENDER CALL - IN LOG | | | | | |
|---|---|---|---|---|---|---|---|
| | | MONTH: _____ | | | | | |

| DATE | CUSTOMER NAME | BANK | AS IS | CONDITION APPROVED | DENIED | APPROVAL REJ. | COMMENTS |
|------|---------------|------|-------|----------|--------|------|----------|
| | | | | | | | |

## Monthly Sales Log

| MONTH | | | | | | | | |
|---|---|---|---|---|---|---|---|---|
| SALESPERSON | RETAIL UNITS | FINANCE | LEASE | SERVICE CONTRACTS | LA & H | OTHER | TOTAL | AVERAGE P.R.U. |
| | | | | | | | | |
| | | | | | | | | |
| | | | | | | | | |
| | | | | | | | | |
| | | | | | | | | |
| | | | | | | | | |
| | | | | | | | | |
| | | | | | | | | |
| | | | | | | | | |
| | | | | | | | | |
| | | | | | | | | |
| MONTHLY TOTALS | | | | | | | | |

Appendix E: Deal Forms

## Income Verification

---

Customer Name_____    Date_____

Please assist us with the items below to ensure accurate and timely processing of the financing on your new automobile. We will need the following by _____

_____ Copy of your 1990 tax return (Form 1040).
Include first two (2) pages, Schedule C (Business Income)
and Schedule E (Rental Income).

_____ Copy of a current pay stub,
showing year–to–date income.

_____ Current registration on trade–in

_____ Title (Pink Slip) on trade–in.

_____ Other:_____
_____
_____

_____ *Please contact your insurance agent on the next business day.
Be sure to tell your agent which bank is financing the car.*

Thank you for allowing us to earn your finance business.
To expedite this process, please feel free to mail or fax the information directly to:

Finance Department
Everyday Motors
222 Shopping Boulevard
Cartown, CA 95123

**FAX :**   (408) 268-0137

_____        _____
Customer Signature                                          Everyday Motors

---

This should be a two-part form. The customer gets a copy and the finance department keeps a copy.

A customer who is procrastinating should be reminded that she agreed, in writing, to provide the necessary information.

The amount of income to be verified should be noted.

167

## Forecasting

### Finance and Insurance Forecast 1992

| Forecast 1991 | Number | Percentage/ Penetration | Dollars per Unit | Annual Gross |
|---|---|---|---|---|
| Contracts | | | | |
| Leases | | | | |
| Service Contracts | | | | |
| LA&H | | | | |
| Aftermarket | | | | |
| Totals (Units) | | P.R.U | | |

| Actual 1991 | Number | Percentage/ Penetration | Dollars per Unit | Annual Gross |
|---|---|---|---|---|
| Contracts | | | | |
| Leases | | | | |
| Service Contracts | | | | |
| LA&H | | | | |
| Aftermarket | | | | |
| Totals (Units) | | P.R.U | | |

| Forecast 1992 | Number | Percentage/ Penetration | Dollars per Unit | Annual Gross |
|---|---|---|---|---|
| Contracts | | | | |
| Leases | | | | |
| Service Contracts | | | | |
| LA&H | | | | |
| Aftermarket | | | | |
| Totals (Units) | | P.R.U | | |

## Telephone Numbers

| Bank | Number | Bank | Number |
|---|---|---|---|
| BMW Retail | 800 662-0269 | | |
| BMW Lease | 800 488-1651 | | |
| Bank of the West | 800 851-5800 | | |
| Chase Manhattan | 800 336-6675 | | |
| Gecal Retail | 800 488-5208 | | |
| Gecal Lease | 800 488-1651 | | |
| Mercedes Benz Credit | 800 547-4260 | | |
| Union Bank | 800 523-9725 | | |
| Volvo Finance | 800 253-8781 | | |
| | | | |
| | | | |
| | | | |

## Contacts:

| Bank | Number | Name |
|---|---|---|
| Bank of America | 800 772-7310 | |
| | | |
| | | |
| | | |
| | | |
| | | |
| | | |
| | | |
| | | |
| | | |
| | | |
| | | |
| | | |

## Insurance:

| Department of Insurance | 415 557-1126 | California office |
|---|---|---|
| | | |
| | | |
| | | |
| | | |

## Daily Finance Log

| R/S # | DATE | STOCK # | NEW/ USED | CUSTOMER | MAKE | MODEL | TRADE | SALESPERSON |
|---|---|---|---|---|---|---|---|---|
| | | | | | | | | |
| | | | | | | | | |
| | | | | | | | | |
| | | | | | | | | |
| | | | | | | | | |
| | | | | | | | | |
| | | | | | | | | |
| | | | | | | | | |
| | | | | | | | | |
| | | | | | | | | |
| | | | | | | | | |
| | | | | | | | | |
| | | | | | | | | |
| | | | | | | | | |
| | | | | | | | | |
| | | | | | | | | |
| | | | | | | | | |
| | | | | | | | | |
| | | | | | | | | |
| | | | | | | | | |
| | | | | | | | | |
| | | | | | | | | |
| | | | | | | | | |
| | | | | | | | | |
| | | | | | | | | |

| MONTH TO DATE TOTAL | DEAL TOTAL | FINANCE RESERVE | LEASE RESERVE | SERVICE CONTRACT | LA & H | OTHER | BANK | NOTES |
|---|---|---|---|---|---|---|---|---|
| | | | | | | | | |
| | | | | | | | | |
| | | | | | | | | |
| | | | | | | | | |
| | | | | | | | | |
| | | | | | | | | |
| | | | | | | | | |
| | | | | | | | | |
| | | | | | | | | |
| | | | | | | | | |
| | | | | | | | | |
| | | | | | | | | |
| | | | | | | | | |
| | | | | | | | | |
| | | | | | | | | |
| | | | | | | | | |
| | | | | | | | | |
| | | | | | | | | |
| | | | | | | | | |
| | | | | | | | | |
| | | | | | | | | |
| | | | | | | | | |
| | | | | | | | | |
| | | | | | | | | |
| | | | | | | | | |
| | | | | | | | | |
| | | | | | | | | |
| | | | | | | | | |

# Notes

# Notes

# Notes

# Glossary

# A

**Acceleration Clause:** part of a contract providing for immediate payment of an entire debt in the event of certain circumstances. For example:
"In the event you fail to pay the installments on time, the company may declare the entire debt immediately due and payable and begin legal action to collect the full amount."

**Amortize:** to provide for the gradual repayment of a debt, usually in the form of periodic payments.

# B

**Balloon loan:** a finance contract with a final payment that is larger than each of the previous payments.

**Bump**: An increase. a raise in payment.

**Bus**: a rogue vehicle that runs rampant through the car business and under which a good many worthy people have been thrown from time to time.

# C

**Charge-back:** that part of the dealer reserve paid to the dealer which is unearned due to prepayment or repossession. The dealer must repay a pro-rated amount at the time the loan is closed.

**Chattel Mortgage:** a legal document used to pledge personal property to another party as security for a debt.

**Closed End Lease:** A lease in which the lessee has no further obligation at lease end. Assuming no more than reasonable wear and tear and no excess mileage, the lessee may return the car and 'walk away'.

**Collateral:** Property that is pledged as security for an obligation. Collateral may be a vehicle, or any sort of equipment, as well as real estate.

**Collision Insurance:** Required to compensate for potential damage to collateral as a result of a collision with property or another vehicle.

**Co-maker:** also called a co-signer or co-borrower. One who joins another in a contract, usually to reinforce credit worthiness.

**Comprehensive Insurance:** Required to compensate for potential fire damage to the collateral, as well as theft, glass breakage or vandalism.

# D

**Dealer Agreement:** the contract between the dealer and a wholesale or retail financing source which stipulates the terms and conditions of the relationship.

**Dealer Reserve:** the income paid to the dealership as the result of a sale of a contract or lease to a lender. It is the difference in charges between the retail rate and the discount rate.

**Default:** the failure to live up to the terms and conditions of an agreement. A borrower is 'in default' from the date all or part of an installment is due and has not been paid, or when other stipulations have been violated.

**De-horse:** a technique to take a customer with a trade-n vehicle off the market until he can take delivery of his new car. The dealership keeps his trade and lends him a car to use.

**Delinquent account:** any account which is currently past due.

**Discount rate**: the rate at which a lender will buy a retail contract from the dealer. Commonly called 'the buy rate'. It is called the 'discount rate', since it is (hopefully) less than current retail rates.

# E

**Empathy:** feeling with. A mental state in which one identifies with or feels in the same state as another.

**Excess Mileage Charge:** a fixed charge (int erms of cents per mile) paid by the lessee for miles driven over and above the stated allowable annual mileage.

**Equity:** The difference between the market value of collateral and the amount owed on the collateral.

# F

**Farmer's contract:** a finance contract which allows for irregular, usually seasonal, payments.

**Finance Reserve:** see dealer reserve.

**Floor Plan:** the financing agreement that subsidizes the new car inventory of a dealership. when a dealer sells a vehicle, he pays the balance due on that vehicle to the bank and receives title, which the dealer then transfers to the customer. the extent to which dealers 'floor' their inventories varies widely.

# G

**Guarantor:** a person or company that guarantees the debt of another party will be paid.

# H

**Highball:** an optimistic trade appraisal.

**Holder in Due Course:** the third party to whom a credit or installment contract is sold.

# L

**Lessee:** the holder of the lease ... the customer.

**Lessor:** the one who 'lets' the property. At first, this is the dealer, then the lease is assigned to a bank and the bank becomes the lessor when the lease is booked.

**Lease:** a contract that allows property that is owned by one party to be used by another party for a specified term and with a specified schedule of payments, including an original value and a termination value.

**Liability Insurance:** the insurance drivers are required to carry in order to provide for expenses caused by harm they may do to another person or the property of others.

**Lien:** a contract or mortgage which holds financed collateral as security against default of payment.

**Limited Repurchase Agreement:** the dealer assigns a contract to a lender with the agreement that the dealer will repurchase the collateral if the buyer defaults. Terms can be negotiated.

**Lowball:** an optimistic price quote to a customer.

# N

**Non-recourse:** a contract endorsement by the dealer that assigns all responsibility for payment collection to the lender. The bank has no recourse to the dealer in the event of default.

# O

**One Pay contract:** a contract containing a clause that gives the buyer an option to obtain other financing after taking delivery of the vehicle. This is not a recommended way to deliver cars, since the customer may return the car if she does not obtain her own financing or rescind the contract at any time during the term.

# P

**Physical Damage Insurance:** insurance protection against collision, fire, theft, glass breakage or vandalism. It is Comprehensive and Collision inurance.

**Pick-up Payment:** a payment which is due after the downpayment and before the regular payments. Rarely used any more and not accepted by many banks.

**Post-dated Check:** a check dated for deposit at a tme later than the date of issue. This is a promissory note, not real money. Don't take wooden nickels or post-dated checks. Both are illegal.

**Promissory Note:** a promise to pay some money at a future time.

# R

**Rapport:** literally ... to carry back. A relationship marked by harmony, conformity, accord or affinity. A mutual understanding.

**Repossession:** collateral reclaimed from a party to a contract who is in default.

**Rescission:** the act of voiding a contract or agreement by restoring the status of both parties to the original condition.

**Residual Value:** the estimated wholesale value of the vehicle at the end of a lease. Usually, the lessee may buy the car for this figure, plus taxes and any fees.

**Rollback:** a sale that is not completed because of lack of financing, buyer's remorse or acts of God. If delivery was made, California DMV requires that license fees be paid.

**Rule of 78's:** a formula for calculating the amount of unearned insurance premiums or finance charges to be refunded to a borrower upon early termination.

# S

**Short Downpayment:** a total downpayment that is less than required by the lender, leaving the amount financed too high for the lender's requirements.

**Simple Interest:** a contract whereby payments for a vehicle are made in equal monthly installments of principal plus interest on the unpaid balance. As payments are made, the balance declines and the monthly interest decreases.

**Spot Delivery:** a vehicle that is delivered to a customer without final payment having been made or without final approval from a financing source.

**Straw Purchase:** a purchase of a vehicle by someone who is actually representing a third party ... usually a third party with questionable credit.

# T

**Termination:** normal termination occurs when a lease expires as originally planned. Early termination occurs when the expires by mutual agreement, usually by a payoff of the outstanding balance, before the originally-stated date.

# V

**Vendor's Single Interest:** insurance that can be obtained by a lienholder to protect an interest in a vehicle being held as collateral, in the event the borrower does not produce proof of insurance. The debt, not the borrower, is insured.

**Voluntary Repossession:** the voluntary return of a vehicle to the dealer or lender by the borrower who can no longer makes payments. Not necessarily OK just because it is voluntary.

# W

**Warranty:** a guarantee that goods or services will be as represented.

# Index

## A

APR to ADD-on rates 159
Abraham Lincoln 41, 123
**Accessories 132**
    appearance package 134
    brochure 135
    display 134
    packaging 132-134
    presentation 132
    presentation book 137
    products 137
    total protection package 136
    binder 15
    coordination with Service 10
    pricing 10-11
    sequence of presentation 5
Accounts Receiveable 9,18
Active listening 98
Agreement Frame 103
Agreement to Furnish Insurance 32
Al Capone 133
Aldous Huxley 43
Alexander G Bell 116
Amortization Schedule 68,70
Andretti 3
Andrew Carnegie 14
Andrew Grove 99
Appearance Package 134
Asking Questions 104-105
Assigning the contract 71
    guarantee 71
    limited repurchase 71
    90 day repurchase 71
    non-recourse 71
Attitude 4, 86, 90, 93
Auditory people 94-96
Authority
    establishing 16
    selling from 88
    vs. control 88

## B

Bandler 106
Bankruptcy 52
Banks: See Working with Lenders 56
Bear Bryant 10

Belief 88, 89, 92, 105, 107
Benjamin Disraeli 52, 115
Bill Klem 97
Bill of Sale 34, 145
Bo Diddley 119
Body Language 98
Brain 89-91
Brochure 135
Business Banker 51, 82
Business Loans 67
**Business Manager 2**
    appearance 14
    professional 23,26,50, 62
    duties 2, 7, 41, 49
    forecasting 20
    introduction 5, 17
    offering a service 41, 132
    personality 3
    setting goals 22
Business Office 3, 9
    relationship with 26
    support for 8
Buyer's remorse 18

## C

Call Log 165
Calvin Coolidge 56
Car and Truck expenses 42, 160
Carlos Castenada 91
Cash Deal 86
    cash conversion 63, 64, 70, 86
    IRS Form 87
    payment in currency 86
    receipt for cash \17
Charge-offs 51-52
Charles Dickens 57
Chekov 107
Chinese proverb 17
Chrysler Plan 81
Closed-end Lease 76
Co-Signer 65
    assisting to qualify 51
    financing with 65
    form 33
Collection accounts 49-51
Commercial Registration 149
Commitment 4

# Index

    in writing    13
Communication    3, 94-99
Computer skills    62
Connecting words    99-100
Consumer Leasing Act    156
Context    4
    as meaning    92
    problem credit    52
Control    27, 88
Conversation    27, 50, 65
Cash customer conversion    64, 70, 86
Corporate Resolution to Borrow    67, 82
Counseling the customer    89
Cover sheet    162
Credit Application    See Customer Statement    40
**Credit Insurance**    **122**
    benefits    129
    commissions    122
    definitions    128
    objections    126
    presentation    124
    prospects    122
    selling intangibles    122
    statistics    125
**Credit Profile**    **48**
    asking questions    27
    buying criteria    49
    collection    49
    debt ratio    42
    decoding    49
    delinquencies    49
    early in deal    41
    Equal Opportuntiy Act    157
    Four C's of Credit    40, 45, 53
    liens    53
    reporting agencies    49
Credit rating    65
Credit Union
    conversion    63
    rate book    15, 63
Customer interview    49-51
**Customer Statement**    **40**
    adding information\\    27
    completing form    45
    early in deal    17, 41
    form    44
    sales meeting    7
    scoring systems    40, 48, 157

# D

DBA    67
Daily Log    15, 170
Dale Carnegie    16, 37, 50, 65, 67, 127, 129
Deal    16
    developing    41
    packaging    8,9
    processing    19
    routine    17, 26
Dealer    2,3,12
Debt ratio    16, 42, 43
Delinquencies    49-52
Delivery    12,16,50
    report of sale    31
Demonstrators    142
Depreciation    42, 160
**Disclosure**
    close on payment date    5
    Consumer Leasing Act    156
    Magnusson- Moss Act    158
    Regulation Z    155
    routine    16, 27
    sequence    5
    Truth in Lending Act    155
Display    134
**DMV Forms**    **142**
    bill of sale    145
    commercial registration    149
    demonstrators    142
    duplicate registration    147
    duplicate title    148
    environmental plates    144
    statement of facts    143, 147
    lien satisfied    146
    name statement    146
    non-resident military    142
    plate interchange    143
    statement of error    145
    title only transfer    149
DMV Secretary    8
    handling forms    30
Documentation
    for lenders    9, 40, 72
    debt ratio    42
    income verification    18
    routine    37

Due Bills     9, 10
Duplicate Registration     147
Duplicate title     148

# E

Earl of Chesterfield     40
Elvis Presley     64
Embedded commands     101
Emerson     12, 82, 106
Employment contract     46
Enthusiasm 27, 79, 106, 112, 123
Environmental Plates     143, 144
Equal Opportunity Credit Act 41, 157
Establishing a credit rating     65
Evidence manual     23, 86
Excellence     3, 18
Expectation     4
Expressed Warranty     158
Eyes     95

# F

**F&I Department     2**
    business card file     15
    call log     165
    daily log     15, 170
    evidence manual     23
    follow-up     18
    forecasting     20, 168
    income verification     18, 167
    monthly log     166
    office     14
    priorities     6
    rate book     7
    retail prices     6
    setting goals     22
    telephone book     15
    telephone numbers     169
    weekly log     164
F&I manager. See Business Manager 2
Fabric Protection     134
Fair Credit Reporting Act     2
Feature the appropriate benefits     92
Feeling people     94-96

**Financing     62**
    APR to ADD-on rates     159
    amortization schedule     68, 70
    assigning the contract     71
    business loans     67
    cash conversion     63-64
    co-signer     65
    computer skills     62
    credit rating     65
    DBA     67
    Financing vs. Leasing     79-80
    guarantor     67
    making extra payments 70
    newsletter     23
    one-pays     66
    Regulation Z     155
    reserve     9, 23
    Rule of 78's     67-69
    sequence of presentation 5
    simple interest     67
    Truth in Lending Act     155
Five year Protection Package  136
Five-liner     45
Floor mats     134
Follow up     18-19
    late penalty form 163
    service contract letter  118
Forecasting     20, 21, 168
**Forms     26**
    signing     26, 27
    needed for a deal     28-34
    Agreement to Furnish Insurance 32
    Authorization for Payoff 34
    Bill of sale     34
    Call Log     165
    Credit Apllication     44
    Daily Log     170
    Forecasting     168
    Income Verification     167
    Insurance Information card   163
    Luxury Tax exemption     151
    Money-back Guarantee 119
    Monthly Log     166
    9 pack     34
    Notice to Cosginer     33
    Odometer statement     29
    Payoff verification     35
    Power of attorney     28
    Recap Sheet     162

Report of Sale 31
Resale card 152
Rescission agreement 161
Service contract cancellation 117
Service contract transfer 117
Tax declaration 152
Weekly Log 164
Francis Bacon 95
Funding 19, 57, 72

# G

Gap insurance 78
George Bernard Shaw 49
Glossary 175
Goals 20-22, 164
Grinder 106
Guarantor 67
Gustav Mahler 26

# H

Hannibal 19
Henry Ford 124
'Hold' checks 86
Husband. See Spouse

# I

I Ching 75, 96
Illusions 90-92
Implied Warranty 158
Incentives 7, 11
**Income Verification 18, 160**
    agreement to provide 18
    bank statements 46
    before delivery 7
    copy of divorce settlement 46
    CPA Letter 46
    depreciation 160
    paycheck stub 46
    financial statement 46

rental agreement 46
request form 167
rescission agreement 161
savings accounts 46
Schedule C 160
Schedule E 160
social security 46
sources 42. 46
tax return 46, 160
Insurance 19
    credit insurance 122
    form 32
    gap insurance 78
    information card 163
    requirements for leasing 77
    verification 7, 19, 72, 87
Irving Berlin 102

# J

Jeffrey Davidson 114
John Lilly 89
John R. Du Teil 46
John Wooden 23
Julius Caesar 100
Julius Fast 98

# L

LA&H. See credit insurance
Larry Bird 20, 62
Laws 150
    Consumer Leasing Act 156
    Equal Opportunity Credit Act 157
    Luxury tax 154
    Luxury tax exemption 151
    Magnusson-Moss Warranty Act 158
    Out-of-state delivery 151
    Regulation Z 155
    Resale card 152
    Sales tax 150
    Tax declaration 152
    Truth in Lending Act 155

**Leasing            74**
    advantages of    83
    assuming         75
    business lease   82
    closed end       76
    common questions    75
    Consumer Leasing Act    156
    conversion       41
    customers        74
    early termination    75
    gap insurance    78
    insurance requirements   77
    leased trade-in  36
    leasing v financing    79-80
    luxury tax       77
    mileage restrictions    76
    newsletter       23
    odometer statement    36
    open end         76
    options at term  79
    payment calculation    78
    rates            75
    residuals        75, 77
    sales tax        83
    tax changes      76
    wear and tear    76
Leather protection    134
Lenders. See Working with Lenders
Lien Satisifed        146
Lienholder            31
Liens                 35, 53
Lombardi              18, 63, 79, 113
Luxury tax            77, 151, 154

# M

Magnusson - Moss Warranty Act    158
Making extra payments    70
Margaret Thatcher    110
Meaning              91-93
Meaning of Life      4, 993
Mirroring            96-97
Models               106
Monthly Log          166

# N

Name statement       146
Names                101
Napoleon Bonaparte 53, 101, 122
Negotiation          71, 74
Neils Bohr           21
Neuro-Linguistic Programming  92
    active listening  98
    agreement frame        103
    auditory people  94
    body language  98
    connecting words       99
    embedded commands    101
    establishing rapport    94
    feeling people  94
    mirroring        96
    reframing objections    101
    using models    106
    using voice      98
    visual people   94
New Testament        78
Nietzsche            112
9 pack               34
Non-recourse         71
non-resident military  142
Notes on notes       13

# O

**Objections        103**
    anticipating     103
    handling         102
    price            103
    reframing        101, 102
    credit insurance 126
    financing        63
    leasing          75
    service contracts    114
Odometer statement 29, 34, 36
Office manager       8
One Pay              18, 66, 163
Open-end lease       76
Out of state delivery 149, 151

## P

| | |
|---|---|
| Packaging accessories | 132 - 137 |
| Packaging deals | 8, 72 |
| Paint Protection | 134 |
| Paperwork | 5, 8, 17, 26 |
| Paul J. Meyer | 128 |
| Paycheck stub | 46 |
| Payment date | 5 |
| Payoff | |
|     difference | 35 |
|     lien satisfied form | 146 |
|     rule of 78s | 69 |
|     telephone numbers | 169 |
|     verification form | 35 |
| Perception | 91 - 93 |
| Personal financial statement | 46 |
| Peter Schultze | 27 |
| Pinstripe | 134 |
| Plans and perception | , 14, 91-93 |
| Plate interchange form | 143 |
| Policy | |
|     from dealer | 12 |
|     one pays | 16 |
|     DMV | 30 |
| Post-dated checks | 86 |
| Power of attorney | 28 |
| Presentation book | 137 |
| **Presentations** | **5** |
|     style of | 27 |
|     accessories | 132 |
|     credit insurance | 124 |
|     financing | 63 |
|     leasing | 80 |
|     service contracts | 112 |
| Price | 5 |
| Products | 137 |
| Profit | 110 |
| Proust | 92 |
| Purchase orders | 16 |

## Q

| | |
|---|---|
| Queen Victoria | 111 |

| | |
|---|---|
| Questions | 104 - 105 |
| Quoting price or rates | 5, 16 |

## R

| | |
|---|---|
| Rapport | 94, 98, 104 |
| Rate book | 15 |
| Recap sheet | 162 |
| Recourse | 71 |
| Reframing objections | 101 - 102 |
| Regulation Z | 2, 155 |
| Report of Sale | 31 |
| Repossessions | 52 |
| Resale | 30, 152 |
| Rescission agreement | 161 |
| Rescission period | 26 |
| Robert Frost | 42 |
| Rock Man | 93 |
| Rockefeller | 7 |
| Rollback | 145, 161 |
| Roosevelt | 2.. 59 |
| Rule of 78s | 67 |

## S

| | |
|---|---|
| **Sales department** | **3** |
|     communicating with | 3, 111 |
|     contribution of | 6 |
|     with accessories | 133 |
|     support for | 7 |
|     training | 45 |
| Sales tax | 150, 153 |
| Samuel Goldwyn | 104 |
| Schedule C | 160 |
| Schedule E | 160 |
| Schopenhauer | 13 |
| Selling | 88 |
|     as a counselor | 89 |
|     as a psychologist | 89 |
|     as a business manager | 3, 4, 97 |
|     asking questions | 104 |
|     handling objections | 103 |
|     modelling | 107 |
|     selling intangibles | 122 |

Seneca 4
Sequence of presentation 5
**Service contracts 110**
    benefits 116
    bumper to bumper 11
    cancellation form 117
    closing 113, 119
    money back guarantee 119
    objections 114
    presentation 112
    price 111, 115
    transfer 117
    waiver 111, 115
    claims 10
    follow up 11. 111, 118
    Magnusson-Moss Act 158
    service drive 10, 111
**Service department** 2
    relationship with 10
    support for 10
    selling accessories 133
Shakespeare 5, 105, 126
Simple interest 67
Sioux proverb 22
Solomon 58
Sound insulation 134
Spouse
    buying alone 41
    Equal Opportunity Act 157
    information 45
    9 pack 34
State of mind 97
Statement of Error 147
Statement of Facts 147
Stevenson 88
Sub-contractors 11, 33
Success 4

# T

Taxes
    declaration form 152
    luxury 77, 154
    luxury tax exemption 151
    non-taxable sales 150
    on leases 83
    resale card 152

    sales tax 150, 153
Telephone manners 19
Temporary registration 7, 30
Timing 4
Title only transfer 149
**Trade in 34**
    authorization for payoff 34
    bill of sale 34
    duplicate registration 147
    duplicate title 148
    leased trade in 36
    lien satisfied 146
    lienholder 34
    9 pack 34
    odometer statement 36
    paperwork 17
    payoff difference 35
    payoff verification 35
    payoffs 9
    plate interchange 143
Trial close 5, 105
    forms as cues 26
    Truth in Lending Act 2, 155

# V

Vanity Plates. See environemntal plates 143
Visual people 94 - 96
Visualization 4
Voice 19, 98

# W

W.C. Fields 125
Warranty
    expressed 158
    implied 23, 158
    Magnusson-Moss Act 158
Weekly Log 164
Will Rogers 15
William Blake 90
William James 8. 86
Winning 62, 63, 93, 113

**Working with lenders 56**
    call log 165
    choosing sources 41, 57
    cover sheet 162
    credibility 42, 56
    credit problems 52
    credit profile 52
    customer statement 44
    debt ratio 43
    developing relationships 56
    funding 57
    grinding 57
    income verification 46
    more grinding 58

Made in the USA
Lexington, KY
19 June 2016